Room Service

James Schofield

(S) Summertown
Publishing

Published by
Summertown Publishing
Aristotle House
Aristotle Lane
Summertown
OX2 6TR

www.summertown.co.uk
email: info@summertown.co.uk

ISBN 978-1-9059-9208-9

First published 2008
Reprinted 2009

Read and produced by David McAlister

Cover by white space
Layout by Rob Hancock Design Ltd

Printed and bound by Times Offset (M) Sdn. Bhd. Malaysia

CONTENTS

Chapter 1

Skim read the chapter once. Check:
- where the Grand Hotel is.
- what Richard does there.
- how old the Grand Hotel is.

It began at ten o'clock on a Friday morning when Elizabeth walked into the bar of the Grand Hotel in Valletta, Malta, and said to the barman:

"Can I have a cappuccino, please?"

"Right ... that'll be 80 cents, please.

"Thanks. Here you are."

"Thank you, and here's your change."

"Thanks."

She left the change on the counter and wrote something down in a notebook.

"Three!" she said to herself. She closed the notebook and smiled at Richard across the bar.

"Is there something wrong?" he asked.

"No, no. I'm doing research. You're British, aren't you?" He nodded. "Well, on average, in a typical conversation like this we say 'Please' twice and 'Thank you' three times. I'm doing a masters degree in anthropology," she explained.

"And that's what anthropologists do, is it? Study people's conversations?"

"Not just conversations! Clothes, food, drink, behaviour ... everything."

Richard wished he was still studying. He had finished his geography degree at university last summer. Now it was May and he was working in the Grand Hotel in Valletta as bellboy, waiter, receptionist, driver ... anything that needed doing really. The manager – Aurora Picardi – was a friend from school. When he visited her after his exams she gave him a job while he decided what to do next. His parents kept asking him when he was going to do 'something sensible'. But what was sensible?

"I'm working on a novel," he said, which wasn't exactly sensible but he hoped it would impress her.

"Really? How far have you got?" she asked.

"It's finished. I just haven't written it down yet, which makes it difficult to sell. That's why I'm still working here. Anyway ... are you staying at the Grand?" Richard asked, to keep the conversation going. Most of the other guests in the hotel were not as easy to look at. She was in her mid-twenties, with long brown hair and large blue-grey eyes. Her nose was perhaps a bit long, he thought, but she had a lovely mouth.

"Yes, I am," she replied. "The manager said my room isn't ready yet. I'm here to see if the Grand Hotel would be suitable for an anthropology conference."

"Right ... well, I'll check to see if your room's ready now, if you like. Your name is ...?"

"Elizabeth Rodgers."

"Richard Villas," they shook hands.

"There!" she said. "We'll probably never do that again. British people don't, you see. The average Briton shakes hands about twice a week. How many times do you think a German shakes hands in a day?" Richard shrugged his shoulders. "Six!" she shook her head in amazement. "Six times every day. Isn't that incredible!"

Aurora was standing at reception with Albert Cini, the head porter, as Richard came out of the bar. Albert was eighty-two and had been employed by Aurora's grandfather as a bellboy when he was twelve. In seventy years at the hotel he had seen and experienced nearly everything. Richard had learnt many useful things from him like how to deal with angry guests, sort out the emotional problems of honeymoon couples, or open locked doors without a key.

"Aurora," Richard called. "Is Ms Rodger's room ready yet? No, no Albert! I can take her bags, don't worry."

"Yes, Maria's just finished the cleaning. Listen, Richard, it's important that we make a good impression on Ms Rodgers," said Aurora quietly. "She's helping to organise a conference and they may use the Grand. So be careful what you show her. We've given her one of the recently-decorated rooms – room 220 – at the front of the hotel, with a view of the sea."

Richard nodded, took the large old-fashioned room key and collected Elizabeth. The Grand Hotel was certainly very grand, but it was also more than a hundred years old. A renovation programme had started and the hotel now had excellent conference facilities, kitchens and reception areas. But some of the bedrooms were not finished and sometimes guests who stayed in the old rooms had a few problems. Two weeks before, a guest needed to be rescued from her bathroom window by the fire brigade when the handle fell off the door. After climbing down the ladder wearing only a hotel towel and a shower cap she was cheered by a small crowd which gathered at the bottom. The local television station even showed it on the news.

They took the beautiful old 1900s lift to the second floor. A lot of new technology was being installed, but Aurora was very careful to make sure that the original Art Nouveau style of the hotel was not lost in the renovation. Richard opened the door to Room 220 and let Elizabeth inside.

It had a tiled floor and a large French window which opened onto a balcony with a clear view of the dark blue Mediterranean sea. The bedroom was painted a plain cream colour and a flat screen television was in one corner. A large black-framed mirror hung on the wall in front of a dressing table and opposite a large double bed, which had patterned Moorish carpets either side of it. A chandelier, made of coloured Venetian glass, hung from the ceiling in the centre of the room. She went onto the balcony and leant on the rail.

"Oh, I love it! Look at the sea! Just think how close we are to North Africa here!" she waved her arm in the direction of Italy. She needs help with her geography, thought Richard. He put her bag down.

"Well, I'll be in reception if you want anything," he said and quickly left.

"Wait!" he heard her call. "Wait!" but he carried on. He didn't want her to tip him.

Chapter 2

Skim read the chapter once. Check:
- what Richard shows Elizabeth.
- who Dr Brian Butcher is.
- what Brian is doing in Malta.

Richard walked downstairs, past Aurora and Albert and into the bar. He picked up Elizabeth's coffee cup from the counter. Interesting girl, he thought. Of course, she probably has a boyfriend somewhere. Maybe even a husband. But perhaps she didn't.

"Richard, how long are you going to stand there holding that coffee cup?" asked Aurora as she came into the bar ten minutes later. She looked at him hard. "Are you all right?"

"Hmmh? Fine, fine," said Richard and disappeared behind the bar to do some cleaning.

Later that morning, Richard was on reception when the lift doors opened and Elizabeth appeared again. He jumped guiltily and dropped the passport which he had been looking through. Albert, who was sitting next to him, picked it up and gave it back to Elizabeth.

"Thank you," she said. "By the way, do you have a map of Valletta? If we hold the conference here I'll need to make a list for the conference delegates of restaurants, bars, museums and other places to visit. Though of course," she added "For most conference delegates a bar is the only place they want to visit"

"Richard could show you around," said Aurora, coming out of her office. "He's an excellent guide to bars and restaurants."

Elizabeth smiled. "Would you mind, Richard?" Richard looked at Albert.

"It's a tough job," Albert replied, "But somebody has to do it. Off you go!" He gave Richard a push and Richard followed Elizabeth outside like a dog let out for a walk.

The city of Valletta was small enough to make a walking tour of the main sites quite short, so when they were finished, Richard borrowed the hotel car and drove to Marsaxlokk to show her the fish market and have some lunch by the sea. They ate mussels cooked in garlic and then fresh fish from the market, grilled in front of them. During lunch Richard listened instead of talking. He didn't concentrate too much on what Elizabeth was saying, but just enjoyed looking at her and hearing the sound of her voice. After a time, however, he noticed that one name was being repeated too often.

"I'm sorry, but who exactly is Brian?" he asked.

"Dr Brian Butcher, my tutor at university. He's really brilliant. He's in charge of the conference. It was his idea for me to come here to check if the hotel is suitable or not." For about five minutes Richard had to listen to how wonderful Dr Brian Butcher was.

"So, he's much older than you, is he?"

"Not really … only about ten years older. I think he's thirty-five."

"So, he's married, then?" Richard continued. Was it his imagination or had

Elizabeth gone slightly pink?

"Yes, that's right," she replied.

Richard relaxed, but only a little. In his experience of university professors, a wedding ring was no guarantee of good behaviour. But, for the moment Richard had Elizabeth to himself and so he decided to show her as much of Malta as possible. They saw the cliffs at Dingli, visited a stone age temple and then took a little boat to see the blue lagoon on the island of Comino. They finally got back to the hotel in the early evening. Richard parked the car and Elizabeth waited for him by the door.

"Thank you," she said. "I really enjoyed myself today."

"My pleasure!" Richard replied. "Listen, if you're not too tired we could go out this eve ..."

"Lizzie! Lizzie! There you are!" A tall thin man was standing at the reception desk waving at Elizabeth. He had thick dark hair and was wearing a cream coloured linen suit which looked very good with his tanned face. "I've just arrived from the airport."

"Brian, what are you doing here?" Dr Brian Butcher gave Elizabeth a kiss on the cheek. "Well, I was going to a seminar at Newcastle University this weekend, but I had a call from the organizers when I was at Heathrow, saying it had to be postponed because of sickness so I bought a last-minute flight over here to see what this place is like. I've just checked into the room next to you."

Richard had doubts. A cream linen suit for a seminar in Newcastle? Even in May and even with global warming, this did not sound very believable. Richard had a feeling he was not going to like the new guest. Brian noticed him standing behind Elizabeth in his hotel uniform.

"Ah ... could you take my bag to room 221? Thanks!"

Richard definitely disliked him.

"Lizzie, shall we get a drink at the bar before dinner?" Brian smiled in Richard's direction, and pushed a small banknote into his jacket pocket.

As Richard saw Brian gently guide Elizabeth in the direction of the bar, he realised he really hated Dr Brian Butcher.

Chapter 3

> **Skim read the chapter once. Check:**
> - where Brian's wife thinks he is.
> - where Brian and Elizabeth go after dinner.
> - why Brian complains about Albert.

It was a bad evening for Richard. He was working in the bar next to the restaurant and could see Elizabeth's face as she had dinner with her tutor. Brian could, it seemed, be very funny and Elizabeth spent most of the meal listening to and laughing at whatever he said.

After a while Albert came and stood next to Richard and watched with him.

"Nice looking girl," he said quietly. "What's she doing with somebody like him? You have to do something, Richard!"

"She's only having dinner with her tutor," Richard replied feeling depressed and dropping peanuts on the floor. Albert looked at him. "And anyway, what can I do?" he continued. "He's good-looking, funny, intelligent, he's got money ..."

"And he's married, isn't he? Come on Richard, you can be quite funny, you aren't stupid and you're much less ugly than me. But if you won't do anything, then I will!"

Just at that moment Brian stood up and walked out into the bar, taking his ringing mobile phone out of his pocket. He ignored Richard and Albert behind the bar and the other guests drinking there and spoke as if he was alone in the room.

"Yes, yes darling ... terrible weather here, but you know, what can you expect in Newcastle! No, no the seminar's going well. Interesting group. Yep, yep ... I'll be back on Tuesday afternoon. I'll call you tomorrow ... yeah, love you too!" Without even noticing his audience, he walked back to Elizabeth. Albert and Richard looked at each other.

"Newcastle!" said Albert "His wife doesn't know he's in Malta. I wonder what that tells us about him, huh?"

Richard thought he knew but didn't want to think about it.

"Can't we stop her drinking?" he complained. "They're half way through a second bottle already." They finished it – far too quickly, Richard thought – and stood up to leave. As they walked past, Elizabeth gave Richard a small guilty smile. He tried to look disinterested, but only managed to look cross.

"I'll tell you what, Lizzie, why don't we get some fresh air? Let's go for a short walk along the sea wall," Richard heard Brian say as they reached the foyer. "Do you want to get a jacket or something? No? Well, if you feel cold, let me know ... you can have mine!" He held the main door open for her, and they went outside. Richard looked at Albert.

"Any ideas?" he asked.

"Close the bar!" said Albert suddenly. "Let's see what we can do." He hurried to the reception desk, checked something on the computer and came back to Richard. "Come on. Upstairs. We have to go to my room. Now!"

Albert had a room on the top floor of the hotel. It had a small balcony and he went outside onto it. There were two chairs, a sun umbrella, a table and an excellent view of the area around the hotel. He left Richard there and returned a moment later with something in his hand.

"Binoculars!" said Richard. "I can't spy on her!" He thought for a moment "Anyway, I won't be able to see very much in the dark."

"Firstly, you *can* spy on her. She needs help," replied Albert "Secondly, these are night glasses, so you should be able to see very well."

Albert carefully scanned the area in front of the hotel, through the night glasses. "Look – there they are!" He pointed to two figures walking along the wall between the hotel and the sea. Brian was, as usual, doing the talking.

"Oh no!" said Richard. "They're going to sit down on that bench." Richard knew the spot very well. It was the perfect bench to choose if you were looking for romance. He had sat on it with a girl himself. It was quiet there, with a beautiful view across the sea and tonight the moon was full and the sky glittered with stars. The moonlight on the water was so strong that they could see a school of dolphins swimming past, bouncing in and out of the water like rubber balls.

Elizabeth jumped up to look at them and through the night glasses Richard saw her turning to Brian and pointing excitedly. He came to join her and used the opportunity to put his arm around her waist.

"What can I do? What can I do? He's going to kiss her!" he moaned. Albert said nothing but got out a mobile phone and started tapping in a number.

"Good idea, Albert, call the police!" said Richard. Albert smiled and shook his head. Richard looked back at the couple. It was about to happen, they were facing each other, Brian leant forward and … and …

And suddenly Brian stopped and pulled out his mobile phone. Albert cleared his throat:

"Good evening, Dr Butcher. Sorry to call at this time. This is Albert on reception at the hotel. I need to know if you would like a newspaper tomorrow morning. We have the *Malta Independent*, or maybe you would like an English paper – the *Daily Express* perhaps?"

Down on the wall Richard could see that the couple had broken away from each other and that Brian was walking backwards and forwards waving his arms. Albert held the phone away from his ear as Brian continued to shout into his mobile and Richard had to put his hand in his mouth to stop himself laughing.

"Right, sir. No paper then," Albert said after a couple of minutes. "Are you sure? Not even the *Daily Telegraph*? All right, I hope I didn't interrupt anything. Good night, sir." He sat back in his chair and put the mobile down on the table.

"He gave his mobile number when he checked in," said Albert. Richard kissed him on the top of his head and jumped around the balcony with excitement. On the wall nobody was kissing anybody. Elizabeth was walking back towards the hotel, her arms tightly crossed across her chest with Brian walking next to her, looking furious.

Richard ran downstairs to be on reception when they came in. He got a tired smile from Elizabeth, a complaint from Brian about Albert and the wonderful sight of Elizabeth running up the stairs to her room, alone.

Chapter 4

Skim read the chapter once. Check:
- what Brian has lost.
- what Richard breaks in Brian's room.
- what problems Richard has with the conference equipment.

Richard arrived early for duty the next morning. Aurora was surprised but pleased to see him.

"That's good … I need your help. Dr Butcher in Room 221 phoned and wants breakfast in his room at nine o'clock. You can take it up. And do remember to be nice to him. He'll decide whether the conference will take place here, not Ms Rodgers. I'm doing a demonstration of the conference equipment for him later this morning."

Richard took the breakfast tray up in the lift and knocked on the door. "Room service!" he called out and went in. Brian was standing in the middle of the room looking through the pockets of his trousers and jacket.

"Put the tray on the balcony," he said to Richard.

Richard laid everything out and came back into the room. Brian had emptied his suitcase onto the bed and was putting everything back, piece by piece.

"Have you lost something, Dr Butcher?" he asked.

"Yes, I can't find my passport. Tell your people to look for it, will you? I must have dropped it in the hotel somewhere."

"Of course, Dr Butcher. Is there anything else I can do?"

"Yes, the shutters in the bathroom are stuck. Can you open them for me?"

Richard went into the bathroom and opened the windows. Honestly, he can't even open the shutters, he thought. What a useless person! He gave the shutters a push.

Then another push …

And then a harder push …

And then there was a terrible noise of wood breaking and Richard watched in horror as both shutters came away from the wall and fell thirty metres into the hotel garden below. There was a bang like a bomb exploding and pieces of wood flew through the air. Richard looked down, hoping that there was nobody underneath. From all sides, windows opened and guests looked out to see what had happened. Brian joined him in the bathroom.

"What have you done?" he asked. "This hotel is falling apart!" Richard ran down the stairs and found Aurora now standing, hands on hips, looking at the damage done to two tables, a sun umbrella and an orange tree in a terracotta pot.

"Was this you, Richard?" she asked crossly. He explained what had happened. "Lucky nobody was hurt," she said. "I'll have to get all the shutters checked this morning. Next time somebody might be underneath. Listen, I don't have time to do the demonstration for Dr Butcher this morning at eleven o'clock now. You'll have to do it for me, OK? This is important so please don't mess it up!" She turned and left.

As Richard collected the broken pieces of wood together he began to feel a little anxious about showing the equipment. He wasn't sure he could remember how it all worked.

When he got to the conference area he found Elizabeth and Brian standing outside waiting for him. Brian had been talking about him.

"Ah, here he is! You're not going to break anything else in the hotel this morning I hope. Lizzie, I think you were probably lucky you didn't have a car crash with Superman here driving you around yesterday." He laughed loudly while Elizabeth looked embarrassed.

Good, thought Richard. He's heard about what we did yesterday and he doesn't like it. "Shall we have a look at the equipment, then?" he asked. They went inside and sat down at the central control panel which was covered in knobs, buttons and dials. Elizabeth and Brian stood next to him. It made him nervous.

"This button here is responsible for opening and closing the electronic shutters," he said, starting with the first thing that he could remember. They all turned to look at the windows. Overhead the multimedia projector hummed into life "... or you can use it to turn on the projector, of course. But if you really want to close the shutters then you press this button here!" Richard pushed at what he thought must be the correct one. Again they all turned to look at the windows. Instead, a large screen came down from the ceiling and the light from the projector shone onto it.

"Right ... well, not that one either then. But anyway, that's not so important. What you are probably really interested in is the video conferencing." He pressed another button and this time the large plasma screen on the wall came to life and an automatic video film about Malta started to play.

"Well done," said Brian. "Finally, got something right! What about the sound?" Richard turned a volume knob, a little too hard. Incredibly loud music filled the room to go with the scene of traditional Maltese dancing on the screen.

"Turn it down, turn it down!" screamed Elizabeth. Unfortunately this wasn't possible. All three of them looked down at the knob which was now in Richard's hand and no longer on the console. The music and dancing were replaced by screaming seagulls flying around fishing boats. In complete panic Richard started hitting the console buttons at random, desperate to make the noise stop. The projector turned from left to right, the screen went halfway up then came back down again, and then suddenly the sound disappeared and the plasma screen went blank.

"Thank goodness!" said Elizabeth. There was a beautiful moment of complete silence.

"You know," said Brian "this hotel and its staff are completely useless. There is absolutely no way I want to run an important conference here with ..." he was stopped by a loud ringing sound from the mobile phone in his jacket pocket.

Chapter 5

Skim read the chapter once. Check:
- why Brian's wife calls him.
- if the conference will take place in Malta or not.
- why Richard is going back to London.

"What is it?" snapped Brian into the mobile. "Oh it's you. Look, darling, can I call you back, I've got a problem to deal with and …" he stopped talking and looked surprised. "The weather?" Again all three of them turned to look at the sunshine pouring through the windows. Brian turned his head away and tried to talk quietly into his mobile. "Well, like I said yesterday it's terrible, but you know, that's Newcastle … What do you mean I'm not in Newcastle? Of course I am … Malta? Why do you think I'm in …" There was then a long silence from Brian and although Richard and Elizabeth pretended not to listen, they could easily hear the sound of an extremely angry woman shouting into Brian's ear. He left the room, ignoring the two pairs of eyes following him.

"Wow!" said Richard, "How did his wife find out he was here?" He put his hand down on the console and accidentally hit a button. They both turned once more to the windows as the shutters went slowly down, the room went dark and Elizabeth began to laugh.

It was, of course, Albert who was responsible.

"Early this morning I went for a walk along the sea wall and I found that somebody had left a passport on the bench. So I took it to the police station and they contacted Dr Butcher's wife because her name was written in the back. And I suppose she was surprised that his passport should be in Malta when he had told her he was in Newcastle."

"But why didn't you bring it back to the hotel?" asked Aurora. "You knew who he was!"

"You know Aurora, my eyes aren't so good these days," replied Albert. "And, as Dr Butcher said last night, I'm just a silly old fool."

"Did he say that?" asked Aurora. "Well he's in big trouble back home. When his wife finished shouting at him he went to the police station to collect his passport and then booked a flight back to London for this evening. I've arranged a taxi for him. Oh, and by the way, he says he's not going to run the conference here and never wants to see Malta ever again. Strange man! What about Ms Rodgers?"

"She's staying until Tuesday as planned," said Richard. "She says she needs a holiday. Aurora, could I possibly have some time off?"

"Time off?" asked Aurora. "After the chaos you've caused today?" she looked at Richard's face which was suddenly full of misery. "Oh, don't be daft. Of course you can have some time off! Just don't do anything dangerous with Ms Rodgers. She hasn't paid her bill yet."

So Richard had two days' holiday and spent the time with Elizabeth. They swam and tried different bars and restaurants and Richard taught her how to catch squid and in which direction North Africa was.

On Tuesday evening he took her to the airport and she flew back to London.

"Aurora," he said next morning. "It's time I went back to London. I need to get a job there."

"Yes," said Aurora "I love having you here, but you should have a proper career. It's more sensible."

That evening he sat with Albert on his balcony and told him what Aurora had said.

"Am I doing the right thing?" Richard asked him "There are so many things I'm going to miss when I leave … you and Aurora for a start, and the weather and the food. "

"Yes," said Albert. "But these things will all still be here for you to visit. And right now you have to follow Miss Elizabeth. That's really the only sensible thing to do."

Chapter 1

Skim read the chapter once. Check:
- if Elizabeth and Richard like their breakfast on Thursday morning.
- when they arrive at the hotel.
- why Mr Segiguchi speaks good English.

It was Thursday morning and Richard and Elizabeth's breakfast in the Hotel Kiyoyama looked exactly the same as the dinner on Wednesday evening.

"What is it?" asked Elizabeth. Richard looked inside the small pot and stirred it with the tip of a chopstick.

"Fish legs," he said finally. "Fish legs in custard. That's what it smells like."

"Don't be absurd. Fish don't have legs," said Elizabeth. "It must be something else."

Richard tasted the end of his chopstick.

"No. It's fish legs … in cold custard."

They looked at each other and Elizabeth pushed the pot to the end of the table where it joined a cold omelette with a line of ketchup down the middle, two small bowls of seaweed-smelling soup, plates with pieces of raw fish and half a rice ball with a plum in the middle which Richard had hoped might be nice. It wasn't.

"Do you think it's just us?" said Elizabeth. "Millions of Japanese eat this for breakfast. Why can't we? I'm sure it's healthy."

"It all comes," said Richard sadly, "From a lifetime eating cornflakes, croissants, rolls, sliced bread, marmalade, jam, tea and coffee for breakfast. Our bodies can't deal with this stuff. It's much too healthy."

Elizabeth looked inside her handbag and found an old piece of chocolate. She gave half to Richard. They were both very hungry.

They were staying in a tiny Japanese fishing village – Kiyoyama – about 100 kilometres outside Tokyo. Apart from a few houses, Kiyoyama had a small Shinto temple, a hotel, a restaurant, a lighthouse and one small shop selling postcards and chocolate bars past their sell-by date. They were there to learn about the 'real' Japan.

"Tokyo's too westernised," the other foreigners at Richard's office had told him. "Get out into the countryside. Try some proper Japanese food, visit a Zen garden, go to some temples. You need to experience real Japanese culture." Elizabeth's Japanese colleagues at Waseda University, where she was finishing her doctorate in anthropology, had said the same only more politely. So Richard and Elizabeth booked a hotel on the coast and travelled to Kiyoyama by train and bus, arriving on Wednesday afternoon.

Their first difficulty was at reception. After five minutes of trying to understand their names, the young receptionist gave up and disappeared into a back office. A few moments later, the manager appeared. He was tall and was wearing a smart black suit, white shirt, white tie and very shiny shoes. He smiled and gave them a deep bow. He was like a large penguin, thought Richard – a large, friendly penguin.

"I'm Mr Segiguchi. Can I help you?" he said slowly and clearly in English.

"We've booked a room until Saturday. Our names are Elizabeth Rodgers and Richard Villas." They showed their passports. Mr Segiguchi looked at the computer. "Ah, your names are wrong on the list. They are difficult names for Japanese to pronounce. " Elizabeth and Richard knew this already from their time in Tokyo. 'Rodgers' was usually turned into 'Wotchus' and 'Villas' became 'Birras'. Generally the Japanese found their first names easier and so they told Mr Segiguchi to use those.

"You speak excellent English, Mr Segiguchi," said Richard politely. "Where did you learn it?"

Mr Segiguchi smiled again. "I worked for a year in London. But I haven't spoken English for a long time. It's difficult now." He shook his head. "You booked half-board," he continued. "The restaurant is closed at the moment because the hotel is empty, but no problem. We can bring food to your room. We have excellent room service. You can try a special Japanese dinner. I will take you to your room now, OK?"

He took them on a tour of the hotel, down silent corridors and past a deserted swimming pool. They only saw a chambermaid who disappeared when she saw the foreigners appear, and a lonely barman who waved at them from behind the counter of the hotel bar where he was polishing glasses. It was like a ghost hotel.

"Mr Segiguchi, why is nobody here? Where are the other guests?" asked Elizabeth. Maybe the restaurant had poisoned an entire conference recently and they hadn't heard about it.

"Guests will all come on Friday for the weekend. There is a big office party. The hotel will be full – cabaret, dancing girls, karaoke – but today and tomorrow, it's only you." They arrived at their room, took off their shoes and stepped onto the straw *tatami* inside. It was clean and light with a sea view balcony and a small bathroom with a shower. On the wall was a long piece of cloth with a *kanji* – a Japanese letter – beautifully painted onto it. Elizabeth looked at it carefully. She was learning Japanese.

"Does that say 'home and family', Mr Segiguchi?" she asked. He was very pleased.

"Ah, Miss Elizabeth, you are right. Not many foreigners take the time to learn our language." Richard felt bad. He found that any Japanese he learnt went out of his head five minutes later.

"Mr Segiguchi, where's the bed?" he asked. Mr Segiguchi slid back the doors of the cupboards.

"You'll sleep on the *futon*. The chambermaid will put it out tonight." He told them what time to expect their dinner ("Many Japanese specialities!") bowed and left.

They unpacked their bags and then went out into the village. They bought some postcards and some chocolate from the shop and looked at the tiny fishing boats, all pulled up on the sand. There was a powerful smell of seaweed filling the air when the wind blew from the beach. Racks of it were drying there before being used for sushi. Across the other side of the bay was a small lighthouse. They climbed past it, sat on the rocks and watched the sun set over the sea. Then it was time to go back to the hotel to try their first Japanese dinner.

Chapter 2

Skim read the chapter once. Check:
- where Richard and Elizabeth eat their dinner on Wednesday evening.
- what they do with the dinner.
- what they do after breakfast on Thursday.

When they arrived the chambermaid was putting the dishes onto a small low table on the *tatami*. She bowed and left the room. Richard and Elizabeth changed into light cotton dressing gowns called *yukata*, put out for them by the chambermaid, then sat cross-legged on cushions and looked at their first meal in a Japanese hotel. There were small dishes with parts of fish that they never thought could be eaten, bowls of different coloured sauces, shiny gold and red fish eggs and slices of something brown and grey which Richard thought still moved from time to time.

"Isn't it beautiful?" he said nervously "It seems a shame to touch any of it."

"It probably will be," said Elizabeth. "Is that thing still alive?"

They took some photographs to show their friends in Tokyo, tried a little bit of everything and then ate some chocolate to take the taste away.

"Oh dear, what will the chef think if we send it all back?" said Elizabeth. "It looks so rude. Can't you eat some more? Try that grey thing again. I think it's sea cucumber. Tim at your office said he liked it."

Richard managed to pick up a slice with his chopsticks, smelt it carefully and then put it down again. Close up it had a powerful smell.

"Tim was lying. We'll have to think of something else."

"Why don't we throw it away somewhere in the hotel?" suggested Elizabeth.

They carefully pushed everything off the plates into a plastic bag and Richard went down the empty corridors, looking for a rubbish bin. He turned a corner and nearly bumped into Mr Segiguchi.

"Ah, Mr Richard!" Mr Segiguchi bowed. "Can I help?" he asked politely. Richard hid the bag inside the large sleeve of his *yukata*.

"Erm ..." Richard tried to think of something. "Erm ... are the hotel baths, the ... erm ... the *sento*, open this evening?" Mr Segiguchi looked surprised.

"Is the shower in your room no good?"

"The shower's fine, but we thought we could try a traditional Japanese bath at this hotel. We read about it in the brochure. It's supposed to be a special feature here."

Mr Segiguchi looked pleased but shook his head. "Today it's closed. Only you and Miss Elizabeth are here. On Friday many, many people will be at the hotel. Then you must try the *sento*. Many Japanese will be happy to see you in the *sento*. I can show you where it is." He led Richard down the stairs to the basement and through one of two doors into a large tiled room with a line of taps along one wall, low down near the floor.

"This is the men's *sento*, Mr Richard. Miss Elizabeth, goes into the ladies' *sento*," explained Mr Segiguchi. "You wash here. When you are clean, you sit in hot water over there." Mr Segiguchi pointed across to the other side of the room where there was a line of square wooden baths.

"It isn't two people in each bath, is it?" asked Richard anxiously. He didn't like the idea of sharing his bath with a stranger.

"No, no, no of course not!" said Mr Segiguchi. Richard relaxed – thank goodness!

"Four people sit together," continued Mr Segiguchi. "More friendly. You can drink *sake* and talk business. But don't worry. On Friday night I can bring you here again and show you."

Richard hoped very much that Mr Segiguchi would forget this idea before Friday. The baths seemed much too small for four people.

They left the *sento* and as his guide went ahead of him down the corridor, Richard dropped the special dinner into a rubbish bin. He bowed goodnight to Mr Segiguchi and went back to the room. Elizabeth laughed when she heard about Richard's conversation. She didn't laugh when she found out she might have to try the *sento* herself on Friday. When they finally went to bed on Wednesday night they were both tired and very hungry. If this was the real Japan, it wasn't much fun.

So on Thursday morning, when the fish legs in custard – or whatever they were – arrived for breakfast, there was only one thing to do. Elizabeth put it all into another plastic bag and they took it with them when they went out of the hotel, carefully hiding it from Mr Segiguchi as they walked past him through reception. They threw it into a rubbish bin near the tiny shop, bought two chocolate bars each, then climbed up the small hill on the edge of the village to visit the temple. They took some photographs of each other to show their friends in Tokyo that they had experienced the 'real' Japan and after about ten minutes were finished. So they went back to the lighthouse to sit on the rocks by the sea.

For a time they watched the ships sailing towards Tokyo. Although the sun was high overhead, a wind from the sea stopped them feeling too hot. They swam, read their books, ate their food and Richard rubbed suntan lotion into Elizabeth's back.

"What about lunch?" asked Elizabeth. "I can't eat any more stale chocolate. Let's try the restaurant."

This time they were luckier. Elizabeth spoke enough Japanese to explain they wanted something cooked, and the owner took them outside to a stall selling fresh fish to the villagers. They chose one, bought it, and he took it into his kitchen and cooked it for them – beautifully. They went back to the hotel for a siesta feeling much better.

Chapter 3

> **Skim read the chapter once. Check:**
> - why Richard is sunburnt.
> - why there is a smell in the corridor.
> - why the chef comes to their room.

"Richard, Richard wake up!" Elizabeth was shaking him. He sat up.

"Ow!" His body was on fire.

"You're badly sunburnt." He went into the bathroom and looked in the mirror. Elizabeth gently rubbed cream into his shoulders. "Richard," she said. "I went down to reception to ask Mr Segiguchi for a hairdryer. There's a terrible smell coming from that rubbish bin in the corridor near the *sento*. If they find that bag they'll know we threw the special dinner away from last night. You've got to get it back again!"

"What? I can hardly walk … why can't you fetch it?"

"Actually, I'm burnt too." It was true that she had a little more pink in her cheeks than usual. Richard, however, looked like a cooked lobster. Elizabeth continued, "Anyway, it's your fault you got so badly burnt. You wouldn't put any suntan lotion on when I told you to and not even a T-shirt although you know it happens every time, but you won't listen. The trouble with men is …"

Richard sighed and carefully put his *yukata* on again – he was not going to win this argument. With stiff legs and moving his body as little as possible, he went out to hunt down the special dinner.

The hotel was starting to come to life as the staff got ready for the weekend guests. In one corridor he saw a group of chambermaids carrying sheets and towels and in another somebody was vacuum cleaning the carpets. Fortunately, there was nobody in the corridor with the rubbish bin. He looked inside; the smell was very powerful. He put his hand down to pick out the plastic bag.

"Mr Richard! Can I help?" Richard jumped around guiltily, banging his sunburnt shoulder against the wall. He stepped backwards, tripped over the rubbish bin and landed on the floor. The rubbish bin fell sideways and the plastic bag landed on Mr Segiguchi's shiny shoes.

"Ouch! Ow!" moaned Richard. "My back, my back!"

"Oh, Mr Richard! Please excuse me!" Mr Segiguchi knelt down and helped Richard to his feet. "Are you all right? The chambermaid said there was a strange smell in the corridor and I came to see what was wrong. Have you lost this?" Mr Segiguchi held up the plastic bag. The smell from the fish was horrible. They looked at each other.

"Mr Segiguchi, I'm so sorry … you see, we … we … tried the special dinner last night and it looked really delicious, but we couldn't eat it. And we thought you and the chef would be upset so I put it in this bag and threw it into the rubbish bin here. But then we could smell it and we knew you would know it was ours, so I was going to take it outside to another bin."

Richard stopped. He felt terrible. Mr Segiguchi wanted to give them a good time and he and Elizabeth just threw away what they were offered. Mr Segiguchi looked upset.

"Please, Mr Richard, it's not a problem. I'll come to your room in a minute!" and with the bag in his hand he hurried off. Richard went back and told Elizabeth what had happened. Just as he finished, there was a knock at the door. Mr Segiguchi and the chef came in. They knelt on the edge of the *tatami* and both bowed to Richard and Elizabeth, who, not knowing quite what to do, bowed back. Then the chef spoke for two minutes while Mr Segiguchi nodded from time to time. Finally, Mr Segiguchi turned to them to translate.

"Mr Sato says he wants to cook a special meal for you tonight. What would you like to eat?"

Richard and Elizabeth looked at each other in surprise. They had expected a telling off. "Is that all he said, Mr Segiguchi? It sounded longer," asked Elizabeth.

"The other stuff is not so interesting. The main thing is, what would you like to eat tonight?"

"Could you say to Mr Sato that we would like some rice and any kind of cooked meat or fish," said Richard. "And please could you say how sorry we are that we didn't eat the food last night."

Mr Segiguchi translated and the chef said something else. "Mr Sato asks what you want for breakfast. He says his brother saw you put your breakfast in the rubbish bin outside his shop."

Elizabeth went as red as Richard and was about to say something but Mr Segiguchi held up his hand. "… and he wants you to know his children eat cornflakes and toast every day. Not so many people eat traditional Japanese breakfast anymore. The taste is … difficult!" Mr Segiguchi smiled, the chef started to laugh, his hand in front of his mouth, and finally Richard and Elizabeth joined in until they all felt comfortable and relaxed again – except for Richard who still found any kind of movement uncomfortable.

The chef and Mr Segiguchi stood up again.

"Mr Sato will go to cook for you. Why don't you visit the hotel bar for half an hour? It's open tonight. Please have a drink on the house."

Chapter 4

Skim read the chapter once. Check:
- what the Filipino women are doing in the hotel.
- who the new guests are.
- whether Elizabeth and Richard enjoy their trip to the sento or not.

To their surprise they were not alone when they got to the bar. Sitting on stools and screaming with laughter were six attractive Filipino women. They were there to do the cabaret performance in the hotel on Friday night. When they saw Elizabeth and Richard they surrounded them with cries of delight and questions. Esmeralda, their leader, spoke excellent English with an American accent.

"I travel around Japan for six months and make enough money in that time to look after my family in Manila for the whole year," she told them. "Back home it's difficult to earn enough to live." The six women found it hard to believe that was exactly the same reason why Richard and Elizabeth had left England to come to work in Japan.

"But you will be here tomorrow, right? You must see our show!" said Esmeralda. They promised to be there and after their drink they returned for Mr Sato's meal, which was delicious – sticks of grilled chicken, cooked shell fish and rice. They went to sleep that night feeling their holiday had finally started.

On Friday morning (after eating enough cornflakes, eggs, toast and coffee for four people) they watched from the balcony as three coach loads of people arrived at the hotel. Mr Segiguchi and most of his staff were outside to greet them. For half an hour he was bowing and organising the guests who climbed out of the coaches and then back in again to find the hats and cameras or bags they had forgotten. And gradually these people, who in their Tokyo offices worked so seriously, began seriously to enjoy themselves. Very soon they were more like groups of noisy, cheerful school children than adult office workers.

The new guests all went to their rooms and exchanged their suits and dresses for *yukata* and wandered around the hotel, the temple, the beach and the village wearing them. From the balcony it looked as if the world had suddenly gone back to a time before technology and global fashions had reduced the surface differences between east and west.

Richard and Elizabeth went swimming again, although this time Richard made sure he was covered up the whole time. He still felt tender and found lying down on the rocks was not possible. So he made a cushion from his towel and sat and watched the ships when he wasn't swimming or reading.

The new hotel guests were as surprised as the cabaret girls to see the two foreigners, but they were shy and didn't try to talk to them directly at first. That changed in the evening when, accompanied by Mr Segiguchi, Richard and Elizabeth went to the *sento*. The men's side was very busy and the wooden baths were all full by the time Richard had finished washing. But a space was quickly made for himself and Mr Segiguchi so that finally four of them sat packed tight together like chocolates in a box and they asked him questions, which Mr Segiguchi translated. Then the other men got out of their baths and came over to listen and ask questions as well until finally the whole male *sento* surrounded Richard, sitting with his knees under his chin in the hot water. It almost felt as if he were being cooked.

When he got back to his room, Elizabeth told him that the cabaret girls had been in the ladies *sento* and shown her what to do.

"It was nice," she said, as she finished her make-up. "But not very relaxing. Imagine being surrounded by hundreds of naked people asking you questions every time you had a bath. You'd never be able to do anything like sing or play with a rubber duck. So, are you ready for the cabaret?"

They were not quite sure what was the correct thing to wear, but the girls had told Elizabeth that the Japanese would wear their *yukata*, so they did the same. Richard found it was the only thing that was comfortable enough. As they went down – Richard still walking slowly and stiffly – the noise coming from the bar was enormous. Two hundred guests were sitting at large round tables eating, drinking and laughing while Japanese love songs came from loud speakers. As soon as the two foreigners appeared, space was made for them at the table nearest the stage at the end of the room and food and sake were put in front of them. They couldn't understand what was said, but in a minute they were part of the group.

After a while Richard had time to look at the stage. A screen and projector were standing on one side and videos – mostly of girls staring sadly at mountains, rain drops on windows, or the sea – played along with the songs. Suddenly, the lights went down, smoke covered the stage, there was a roll of drums and the cabaret began.

The cabaret girls were transformed. In their high heels and sparkling costumes they were much larger than in real life and for the next hour Richard and Elizabeth forgot everything else as the girls did their show. After each song they went behind a screen and reappeared a moment later in another wonderful costume. The guests applauded everything while continuing to eat, drink and chat with each other.

Finally, Esmeralda came to the front of the stage, wearing a short grass skirt and a necklace of flowers. She spoke in Japanese to the audience and two young men were pushed up by their friends onto the stage. Esmeralda said something else and the spotlights started searching the audience. Elizabeth saw what was coming and grabbed Richard's arm:

"Run!" she said, "Run!"

Chapter 5

Skim read the chapter once. Check:
- what Richard and Elizabeth do with the cabaret girls.
- what Richard sings.
- whether Elizabeth and Richard enjoy their holiday or not.

It was too late. As they stood up to leave, the spotlights caught them. There was a cheer from the audience and hands pushed them forwards to the stage. Esmeralda hurried them behind the screen and they were instantly surrounded by the girls who tore their yukata off, fastened grass skirts around their waists and put a grassy bikini top onto Elizabeth and a flowery necklace around Richard.

"Here, take these!" Esmeralda pushed maracas into their hands, "Stand behind me and copy my dancing. Go!"

Before they had a chance to say anything the screen was gone and they were on stage again. Hawaiian sounding music started and Esmeralda and two of the other girls sang, swinging their hips and shaking the maracas in time to the beat. The other girls were in the second line with Elizabeth, Richard and the two young Japanese men. Richard concentrated on trying to imitate Esmeralda's hips as they moved from side to side, and shake his maracas at the same time. Suddenly, the three front girls turned and walked back towards them.

"Keep dancing!" whispered Esmeralda at them as she went past and then Richard and Elizabeth were at the front, still moving from side to side as best they could with an audience that was clapping and laughing hysterically. It was the longest minute in Richard's life but suddenly it was over and Esmeralda was telling the crowd to give a big round of applause. They stood and whistled and stamped and cheered as the dancers bowed and bowed and bowed again. Finally they let them all go to change back into their yukata and return to their tables while Esmeralda started the karaoke machine.

For the rest of the evening the audience came up to them to shake their hands or practise some English or give them more to eat and drink. Elizabeth danced with the managing director of the company twice and the other executives stood in line so that they could have a turn. Richard sang 'Yellow Submarine' with the karaoke machine five times and was about to sing it again when Elizabeth took the microphone away from him and gave it back to the girls. She took Richard by the hand and guided him back to their room, Richard still shaking a maraca which he had forgotten to return. He lay down in the dark on the cool *futon* and was asleep before Elizabeth had even finished taking off her make-up.

Richard woke next morning to the sound of the waves on the beach and a headache. Elizabeth was sitting on the balcony in the morning sun drinking some tea and Mr Segiguchi – perfectly dressed in black suit, white shirt and tie as always – was standing in front of him.

"Mr Richard! Can I help?"

"Mr Segiguchi," said Richard in a weak voice. "I don't think anyone can help. I think I want to die." Mr Segiguchi offered him a glass with something brown and sticky in the bottom.

"Try this. It helps cure hangovers. Hold your nose – bad smell – just drink!"

Richard did as he was told. It tasted disgusting, but it worked. Mr Segiguchi put the breakfast on the table on the balcony and Richard managed to join them. He sat smelling the sea air and gradually felt life returning to different parts of his body. Mr Segiguchi bowed and left.

They had to return to Tokyo in the afternoon. It had been a strange holiday, and not what he had expected at all. All the other foreigners they knew in Tokyo told them the 'real' Japan was temples, flower arranging and the tea ceremony. Maybe that was a part of it, but Richard now thought there was more to Japan than those traditional things. He liked the way they had been accepted into the group in the cabaret and how everybody who sang that evening was cheered and clapped. In Japan it seemed it was better to contribute something – however bad – rather than not contribute anything at all.

"How's your sunburn?" asked Elizabeth. "You're still quite red."

Richard stretched his arms over his head and smiled. "Much better, thanks. The moment we got up on stage I forgot all about it. What an amazing experience that was last night!"

"Yes," said Elizabeth. "Now, I think *we* can tell the people in Tokyo something about the real Japan."

Chapter 1

> **Skim read the chapter once. Check:**
> • where Richard and Elizabeth have landed.
> • what Richard's problem is.
> • which hotel they choose.

Richard and Elizabeth stood and stared at the hotel list while the rest of the airport arrivals hurried off to their sensibly pre-booked destinations.

"Hilary said it was the best way to get a cheap hotel room ... see what's on the airport hotel list when we arrive and give them a call," said Elizabeth.

This idea had sounded good in London but now, ten hours later in Kuching airport on the east Malaysian island of Borneo, Richard Villas was tired and hungry and wanted to know where he and his wife Elizabeth were going to sleep that night.

"Hotel Luk Kwong?" he suggested. "Or how about the Hotel Oriental Garden?"

"Hmm ..." Elizabeth shook her head. "I'm not sure."

They were on a business holiday. A holiday because it was February in London and both of them needed some sunshine and business because Elizabeth was going to have an interview at the University of Kuching.

"Look!" she said. "Brooke's Hotel!"

"Brooke's Hotel? That famous place? Isn't it expensive?"

They had to be careful with money. Neither Elizabeth's job in the anthropology department of the University of London, nor Richard's at an advertising agency, were well paid. Two years before, he thought he would be able to stop work when his first novel was published. But although the newspaper critics loved it, the public didn't. So he stayed at the advertising agency and started work on novel number two.

"No, no, look at the price. That's not too bad!"

"It's still twice as expensive as the other hotels."

"Yes, but Brooke's Hotel, Richard! It's not often you get the chance to stay somewhere like that, is it? And we'll be safe there, don't you think?"

This was an important point because Richard had a problem more serious than not having much money. Cockroaches. It wasn't rational, he knew. They were smaller than him, they didn't bite and they ran away when you turned on the light, but Richard was terrified of cockroaches.

And the cockroaches knew he was afraid of them. Every time he had to go on a business trip somewhere hot they came out to greet him. Even Singapore – where every other form of life whether it had two, four, six, eight or zero legs was carefully organized into its own tidy corner – the cockroaches came to look for Richard. He found one sunbathing on the centre of his towel next to the hotel swimming pool. When Richard saw it he jumped backwards and pushed a passing waiter into the swimming pool. A second went to sleep early one morning in his shoe. He only found it in the evening. The hotel doctor had to give him a tranquillizer.

But this time he wasn't going to let them chase him away. Elizabeth's interview meant too much. A three-year grant from the anthropology department of the University of Kuching for her to study the Kokketti, a tribe of practically stone-age people in the interior of Borneo, with enough money so that he could give up his job and finish his second novel. The plan was that during the week she would study the Kokketti in their village and come back at the weekend to the house on the university campus in Kuching. She had to get the job and he had to learn to live with the cockroaches. But it would be difficult, so it was important that they stayed in a good hotel that was unlikely to have very many.

"Richard, we'll take a bus into town instead of a taxi. That'll save some money."

She telephoned the hotel, booked three nights in the most expensive (even with an extremely good discount) hotel in Kuching and then asked the hotel receptionist for bus directions from the airport. She finished and turned to him.

"Come on, it's just twenty minutes on the bus. He told me it leaves in ten minutes!"

As they stepped outside the air-conditioned airport building, the tropical heat fell on them like a blanket, so by the time they reached the airport bus fifty metres away Richard could feel lines of sweat running down his back and their suitcases felt twenty kilos heavier.

He looked down the inside of the bus carefully, his eyes going from side to side. Elizabeth looked over her shoulder at him. "Have you seen something?" she asked after a moment.

"No ... no. I'm just making sure." He went and sat next to her. She took his arm.

"Remember what Hilary said. She didn't see any cockroaches in five years in Kuching. We'll be fine."

Richard nodded, but didn't feel much happier. Elizabeth's friend Hilary wore glasses thick enough to bullet-proof a window. But she still had problems finding her own bicycle if there were too many parked closely together at the university.

The bus set off. On both sides of the road was thick jungle. The leaves were emerald green and just washed by the afternoon rain so everything shone. As they stopped to pick up some more passengers, Richard saw three monkeys jumping from one tree to another. Sometimes there were little houses near the road with children and chickens running around outside while mothers and grandmothers sat on the steps dressed in beautiful blue, green, red and yellow batik dresses. After the grey skies, streets and offices of London, Richard felt as if he was able to see in colour again. He started to relax. If Brooke's Hotel was clean and cockroach-free, this was going to work.

Chapter 2

> **Skim read the chapter once. Check:**
> • what Brooke's Hotel was originally.
> • what Richard sees in the corridor.
> • where they eat supper.

"Look! What an amazing hotel!"

Brooke's Hotel was a beautiful white colonial building, built in the 19th century as headquarters for the Borneo Trading Company Ltd. It was turned into a hotel in the 1920s and so many famous writers, actors and politicians had stayed there over the years the guide books couldn't list them all. A Sikh doorman with a brilliant white turban, a bright blue jacket with gold buttons and white gloves opened the doors for them. Inside it was cool and dark after the bright sunshine outside. The floor was dark wood, polished so much it reflected the chandelier above and the old portraits of the 19th century company officials on the walls. Their eyes watched Richard as he and Elizabeth crossed the floor to the reception desk. He wished his trainers didn't squeak so much on the shiny surface. They sounded much too 21st century. The receptionist smiled at them.

"Sir? Madam? Can I help you?"

"We called from the airport – Richard and Elizabeth Villas. We reserved for three nights." They handed over their passports, filled in registration forms and went with the porter to their room. The lift stopped on the second floor and the porter went down a corridor which formed one side of an open courtyard.

"You know, I think this was a really good idea to…" Richard suddenly stopped talking. On the dark floor of the corridor was something black … mouse-sized but cockroach shaped. Elizabeth hadn't seen anything yet; she was still putting passports into her bag. At that moment, not making a sound was the only thing that Richard could do.

"Are you all right?" asked Elizabeth. "You've gone white!"

Richard decided not to say anything. She must get the job. She mustn't worry about him. He would deal with it. "Fine, fine. Just tired. Let's take the other side of the courtyard," he said.

"Why? The porter's gone that way."

"Yes, but we can reach our room this way too … and … and I want to see the courtyard from over there. See? Just look at those … those flowers!" He pulled her along behind him to the room, tipped the porter and sent him away.

"Well, this looks nice, don't you think?" said Elizabeth looking around. Overhead a large fan turned above the dark mahogany furniture. Next to the French windows was a sofa, covered in colourful cushions with little mirrors in them that reflected spots of light around the room. They went onto the balcony and looked into the large hotel garden with its green lawns and little paths between clumps of bamboo and tall trees. It was beautiful.

"I'll check the bathroom," said Richard.

"Are you sure? I could do it."

"No. I'll go. I have the problem … not you." He opened the door quickly and put his head inside. Nothing. Elizabeth walked in behind him.

"I'm having a shower, then we'll go out for dinner. All right?"

They went out to eat in the food stalls that night. It was what Richard liked best about the Far East. He loved the different smells and the way the food was cooked in a wok or on a grill in front of you. And there was so much to choose from. There were Chinese, Malay and Indian food stalls with grilled fish, satay or curries and then all the different fruits. Tiny sweet bananas, star fruit, rambutans and – of course – durian. The smell of durian was strange. If you liked it, it smelled rich and sweet. If you didn't, it smelled like old dead meat. They moved from stall to stall, ate and drank lots of everything, talked to the friendly local people eating with them and looked at the stars in the warm tropical sky.

And he didn't see a single cockroach. There was a moment when Elizabeth moved suddenly away from one of the stalls to another. He asked if she had seen a cockroach but she said no, she just wanted to try some of the durian at another stall. Finally they walked slowly back. Brooke's Hotel shone in the moonlight and with its glittering lights and columns looked like a large wedding cake; it was a perfect evening.

"It would be …" "Wouldn't it be …" – they both spoke at the same time and laughed.

"Go on, what did you want to say?" asked Richard.

"Well, it would be wonderful to live here, don't you think?" said Elizabeth. "Not to have that cold wet London weather all the time, not to have to travel with a million other people on the underground every day, not to have pay so much rent for our flat each month."

Richard thought about his job. At the moment his company did advertisements for a new drink called Love Cola and he wrote slogans for the pictures of beautiful young people, slogans like "Open Love! Love life!" His bosses thought he had a great future in advertising. He knew he was wasting his time – his heart was not in it. This could be a chance for them both.

"Yes," he said. "That's just what I was thinking."

Chapter 3

> **Skim read the chapter once. Check:**
> - how Richard kills the cockroaches.
> - who Charles Brooke was.
> - what Richard thinks of the hotel restaurant.

When they returned to the hotel he checked the corridor – nothing. The bathroom – all clear. They brushed their teeth, turned off the light and went to bed.

"Elizabeth?" he whispered after about ten minutes. "Elizabeth?" Her steady breathing told him she was already asleep. Very quietly, he got out of bed, went to his suitcase and took out an insect spray that he had hidden inside a pair of socks. *Roacherize*, as it was called, was illegal in all European countries and many states in the US as well, but a friend had sent it to Richard from Texas and he found it was very effective for dealing with his enemy. Elizabeth did not like it at all, saying the spray was illegal for a very good reason – it was probably poisonous to people as well! So Richard had packed it without telling her. Very quietly he went to the bathroom and sprayed it in all the corners.

"Just in case," he thought as he went back to bed again, "Just in case."

Feeling really safe for the first time since landing in Kuching, he went to sleep.

About two hours later a sound woke him. It came from the direction of the bathroom. He could hear little noises from there, little scratching noises which stopped and started. He lay for a moment feeling the panic inside him. Should he wake Elizabeth? She was always a good sleeper and after the long flight she was exhausted; she hadn't heard anything. Anyway, he couldn't send her in there; he'd have to look himself. Once more he got out of bed, but this time he picked up a newspaper, folded it and went to the bathroom door. He listened again. Yes, something was moving in there. He took a deep breath, opened the door, turned on the light and put his head around the door. Straight away he pulled his head back, shut the door quietly, put the newspaper in his mouth and bit it very, very hard.

Floor, sink, lavatory and bath were all covered in the dead and dying bodies of cockroaches, lying on their backs waving their legs in despair at the ceiling. Richard realised his mistake. *Roacherize* attracted cockroaches and then killed them. By spraying so much he had probably called them together from all over the hotel to his bathroom for a midnight party – with a deadly hangover. He would have to deal with them before Elizabeth woke up.

Later Richard thought this was probably the worst half hour of his life, but finally it was over. He found a brush and dustpan, swept the bodies together and threw them out of the bathroom window into the bushes below. He went to the door and looked around one last time. Everything was clean. He was just about to go when he heard a little scratching noise again. There, on the outside of the bathroom window was a very large dark, mouse-sized cockroach, very similar to the one he had seen earlier in the corridor. It was very much alive and looking straight at him. Richard turned off the light, shut the door and ran back to bed. It was a long time before he fell asleep.

When he finally woke up the next morning at ten o'clock, Elizabeth was gone. She left a note to say that she was shopping and would come back at lunch time. He looked inside the bathroom. Nothing. Good. Perhaps he wouldn't have any more trouble.

He washed, had breakfast and explored the building. It was more like a museum than a hotel. There were photographs of the second White Rajah of Sarawak, Charles Brooke and his beautiful wife, the Ranee Marguerita from the 1870s. In glass cabinets were old weapons from the times of the head hunters and ivory bracelets. The library had books full of pictures of tropical birds and flowers and on the walls were the heads of animals shot by the old white masters of the country – even a small tiger. Richard was sure he could use this in his novel and after a time he decided to sit down in the foyer to wait for Elizabeth and write some notes. He was so busy that he didn't see her when she first came in until he heard her voice as she asked at reception if he was in his room. She seemed very pale, as if she had had a shock. But then most people who lived in London looked very pale when they first arrived in the Far East.

"Are you all right?" he asked. She jumped at his voice.

"Fine, fine … I bought some nice things. Do you want to see?" They went back to the room and she tried them on.

"Shall we go out to lunch?" he finally asked after she had tried all possible combinations of the new items with the clothes she already had. "I read about a really good Malay restaurant near the river that we could go to."

"Ah. Can't we try the hotel restaurant? I … I want to do some work this afternoon, to prepare for the interview tomorrow. And I like it here. There aren't any cockroaches or anything." Richard didn't say anything but was a little disappointed and even more so when he saw the restaurant menu. It was like an old-fashioned English menu from the 1930s. But Elizabeth seemed happy as they sat in the nearly empty dining room with the large ceiling fans slowly turning over their heads and one Chinese waiter of about ninety.

"I expect the old colonialists wanted food to remind them of home," she said. "The chef has probably been working here since then." It was an interesting idea and Richard decided after lunch he would go and talk to the chef. He might make good material for his novel.

Chapter 4

> **Skim read the chapter once. Check:**
> • why Richard goes to the kitchen.
> • who he meets there.
> • what happens to the chef.

Richard left Elizabeth in their room with her papers and a language course – *Kokketti for Beginners* – which she hoped was going to teach her enough to communicate with the tribespeople. Richard was interested to see that in the vocabulary lists at the back of the book there were twenty-five words for rat, but nothing for cockroach. Perhaps they didn't have them in the jungle, he thought. Maybe he could stay in their village instead of the university campus, and while Elizabeth did her research he could write his book or go hunting with the men.

He went outside for a while to the hotel garden. Several of the older guests were sitting in the shade of large betel nut palm trees. He sat down with them, watching tiny brightly-coloured birds flying in and out between them, collecting nectar from the orchids, bougainvillea and gardenias that grew everywhere. How nice to live with this around you all the time instead of the dark, damp grey of London, he thought. Richard was determined; the cockroaches were not going to drive him away. He stood up and went back into the hotel to look for the chef.

The kitchen he walked into was very white and clean, with long stainless steel tables down the middle, cooking surfaces and ovens on the left with the chef's collections of pans, bottles and spices, while the refrigerators hummed quietly to themselves on the right. At the far end the cups, plates and glasses were piled up ready for the waiters to put on the tables and a door led outside to the rubbish bins.

"Hello?" called Richard. "Hello?" Nobody was there. He walked down to the back door and looked outside. Nobody there either. Oh well. He could interview the chef later. He stopped for a moment to look at the different spices next to the cookers. He hadn't tasted any of these in the lunch they had just eaten. Perhaps the chef only used them when he was cooking for the hotel staff. He suddenly felt as if somebody was looking at him so he guiltily put down a bottle of chilli sauce and turned around. "I'm so sorry," he started, "I was looking for ..."

There was nobody there, but as his eyes dropped to the floor he realized that he had a much, much bigger problem to deal with than an angry chef. At ground zero level in front of the refrigerators and ready for action was – again – the mouse-sized cockroach. They both stared at each other. She (Richard had read about his subject – the females were usually bigger) was nearly black and seemed even larger than last night. Very slowly, he picked up a large frying pan from the top of the cooker. She bent her legs and with a sudden jump flew straight at him. Richard was waiting for this and with a blow that a tennis professional would have been proud of, hit her with the frying pan. Cockroach and, unfortunately, frying pan flew across the room straight into the piles of plates and glasses at the far end of the long row of tables. The noise was deafening, but Richard didn't notice. He was watching for movement. Cockroaches, he had read, could survive nuclear war. A frying pan – even a big one – might not be enough.

Without taking his eyes off his enemy, he felt behind him for more weapons and with the bottle of chilli sauce in one hand and a large kitchen knife in the other he moved slowly towards the body. She was lying on her back with her legs in the air on the table. He stopped about two metres away and waited, weapons ready for anything … or nearly anything. Suddenly she jumped to her feet and with incredible speed threw herself onto the floor so that the kitchen knife in Richard's right hand just missed her head and destroyed the last few plates instead. She flew across the kitchen and landed on the wall opposite him above the door. Without thinking Richard threw the bottle across the room. It smashed on the wall next to her just as the kitchen door opened and the chef came in to receive a face full of hot spicy sauce. As he staggered from side to side trying to clean the blinding chilli from his eyes, Richard escaped out of the back door. This was not something he wanted to explain.

About two hours later Richard thought it was safe to return to the hotel. He had bought himself a complete set of new clothes and had his hair cut very short so if the poor chef had actually seen anything before the chilli hit, it would be difficult to connect him with the madman in the kitchen. Nevertheless he kept his sunglasses on as he crossed the entrance hall. The doorman and receptionist smiled but the portraits looked at him as if to say that they knew all about him.

He found Elizabeth fast asleep on the bed, *Kokketti for Beginners* next to her head.

"Nice clothes," she said, rubbing her eyes. "Not sure about the haircut, though. Isn't it a bit short? You look like a criminal." Richard decided it was not the right time to explain how correct that description was.

"What about dinner?" he asked, quickly changing the subject. "We could go to that restaurant I told you about next to the river." Elizabeth looked uncomfortable.

"Well, next to the river there might be lots of cockroaches, don't you think? Why don't we eat here again – the food might be better in the evening."

"We didn't see any cockroaches last night at the food stalls. And I didn't see any when I was shopping. Anyway, I think the hotel kitchen might be closed this evening. The chef had some sort of accident this afternoon. Nothing serious but, umm, he won't be able to cook today."

Finally she agreed, but insisted on taking a taxi there and back. Even then, she pulled him quickly into the restaurant when they saw a cat walk past with something in its mouth as they got out of the taxi. The taxi driver had to come into the restaurant to ask for his money. How sweet that she worries about me, thought Richard. A nice change as well. He remembered that when he had told her about the cockroach in his shoe in Singapore she had laughed.

Chapter 5

> **Skim read the chapter once. Check:**
> • who/what Richard dreams about.
> • what Richard drinks on his balcony.
> • whether Elizabeth accepts the job or not.

That night, as Richard slept, his enemy returned. She was gigantic now, and chased him and Elizabeth from room to room in the hotel on four legs, her two front legs holding a tin of *Roacherize* and a copy of *Men's Health* magazine. He was finally trapped in the bathroom; she sprayed him, he couldn't breathe, something was stopping him ... he woke to find it was morning and he had the sheet over his face.

Elizabeth came out of the bathroom half-dressed. "Are you all right? During the night you kept on mumbling about chilli sauce. What was that all about?"

"Just a dream, just a dream." He lay back exhausted.

"Listen, I'm going up to the university now, OK? I'm not sure what time I'll be back, but I expect it'll be after lunch."

"Right, right. Good luck. See you later." She left and Richard lay for a while thinking about what to do. Staying all day at the hotel was not a good idea. He dressed quickly and went out.

He had a wonderful time. The old part of Kuching was small enough to explore on foot and the temples, churches, cemeteries and waterfront took his mind off his troubles. In a street market he bought himself and Elizabeth fake Rolex watches, and fake Louis Vuitton handbags for his two nieces back in London. He loved the shops with their brightly-coloured batik clothes and strange looking Chinese medicines on display in the windows. He bought a small statue of a Buddha in an antique shop and spent half an hour discussing Manchester United with the owner who was wearing a shirt with "Rooney" on the back. Yes, he thought to himself, he could happily live here. He had lunch sitting outside a small restaurant with a view of the Sarawak River, watching the small painted fishing boats sailing past, writing the occasional line in his notebook about the people around him.

Feeling full of good food and at peace with the world he walked back to the hotel. He decided to sit on the balcony in their room, drink something cool and look at the garden until Elizabeth came back. It was the perfect way to spend the afternoon. As he entered the hotel even the portraits seemed friendlier ... not smiling, but they didn't look at him with their normal dislike.

Richard opened a bottle of cola – Love Cola, he noticed – and stood on the balcony. He looked at his slogan on the side of the bottle – 'Open Love! Love Life!' How nice not to be in the office. He thought about his colleagues back at the advertising agency and how little he missed them; Jackie with her irritating laugh, Tony with his boring stories of what he had done at the weekend and Kevin who always smelled of cigarettes. He took a sip from his bottle, it was so peaceful. The tall trees in the garden moved from side to side in the gentle wind. The blue sky had some big clouds coming closer which would wash the city clean again at 4.30pm, as happened nearly every day. He hoped – he really hoped – that Elizabeth was offered the grant. He could do this for the rest of his life.

Richard sat down in the comfortable chair on the balcony. He rested the bottle on his full stomach and looked up at the bottom of the balcony above his head. There he saw a large black shape moving quickly towards him.

He threw himself to the floor, covering himself with Love Cola, just as the cockroach dropped off the ceiling onto his chair. He rolled into the bedroom, slammed shut the shutters and the windows, drew the mosquito nets and the curtains, and finally moved the sofa in front of everything. He sat there panting. That was it! He had to leave Kuching immediately, it was the only possible thing to do. Everyday she would be out there looking for him, hunting him. But what if Elizabeth got the university grant? He went into the shower to clean off the cola and thought about how to explain his problem. He had no idea what he could say that anyone could understand or believe. He came out of the bathroom to find Elizabeth sitting on the edge of the bed waiting for him.

He sat down on a chair opposite her. Somehow she didn't look very happy.

"Well? How was the interview?" he asked.

"They offered me the grant."

"Ah. Well ... well ... that's great. Isn't it?"

"Yes. Only ... Richard, how important is it for you to give up your job?"

"My job? Well, it would be nice for me of course, but to go and study these people is what you wanted, isn't it?" Elizabeth swallowed and looked at her shoes.

"Would it matter to you if we stayed in London?" she asked. She looked as if she was about to cry.

"Well, it's funny you should say that ... but why have you changed your mind?"

Elizabeth burst into tears and threw herself onto the bed. "Watzz!" she said through a mouthful of pillow after about five minutes. Richard sat next to her and lifted her face up.

"Could you say that again in English? I haven't studied Kokketti as long as you."

"Ra ... ra ... rats!" she repeated, still sobbing. "I only found out today from the professor who interviewed me. The Kokketti have a whole culture based on rats. They worship them, they feed them, they play with them, and they eat them. That's why the language has twenty-five words to describe different kinds of rat. And ever since we've arrived all I've seen every time we leave the hotel are rats, rats, rats. Rats at the food stalls, rats when I went shopping and even that cat last night had one in its mouth. And we thought the problem would be your cockroaches and you haven't seen a single one!"

"Well, that's not quite ... but, anyway, why didn't you say anything before?" asked Richard.

"I know how much you want to leave advertising and write full-time. But I can't bear rats. I can't go and live in a village full of them! I'm sorry, so sorry."

Richard thought for a moment of not saying anything about what had happened to him, but decided that wouldn't be very nice so he told her the whole cockroach story from beginning to end.

"And you really think this one particular cockroach is after you?" she asked finally.

"I *know* she is!" He answered.

"How big is she do you think? This size?" she held up her thumb and forefinger. He nodded. "Very dark?" He nodded again. Elizabeth went over to the bin and picked out a book. Squashed on the back of it was a familiar black shape.

"When I came in I found her waiting for you on the bedside table. I think it was the best thing to do with *Kokketti for Beginners*, don't you?"

ROOM SERVICE – EXERCISES

Chapter 1

① Scanning

Read the chapter carefully. Answer these questions:

1 What does Elizabeth study?
2 Why is Elizabeth staying at the Grand Hotel?
3 What is the name of the head porter?

② Key vocabulary

Match the words to their explanation.

1	change	a	the way that somebody acts
2	counter	b	the right thing/place
3	behaviour	c	coins you get back when you buy something
4	bellboy	d	covered in tiles
5	impress	e	to put something in place
6	suitable	f	place where you pay or are served in a shop
7	install	g	to give somebody a small sum of money for a service
8	tiled	h	to make somebody think well of you
9	rail	i	metal bar fixed around a balcony
10	tip	j	young man who carries bags or messages in a hotel

③ Word partners

Join the word partners in the columns below together. There might be more than one possibility.

1	on	a	facilities
2	shake	b	off
3	sort	c	average
4	make a	d	brigade
5	conference	e	on
6	reception	f	out
7	fire	g	area
8	fall	h	screen
9	flat	i	good impression
10	carry	j	hands

④ Practice

The letters in the words and word partners in italics are in alphabetical order. Rewrite them so they make sense. They are all from exercises 2 and 3.

a) Did you know that *no aaeegrv* every adult European drives 60,000 kms a year?

   _____ _____

b) My old boyfriend drove a Porsche. He bought it to *eimprss* me, but it didn't.

   _____

c) I read that the British government has *adeillnst* more video cameras in public places than the Chinese government.

   _____

d) I can't go to the party. I don't have anything *abeilstu* to wear.

   _____

e) I don't think you should stand on a chair. You might *afll ffo*.

   _____ _____

f) I didn't give the waiter a *ipt* because he didn't bring me back the right *aceghn* when I paid the bill.

   _____ _____

g) For the seminar we need a hotel with good *cceeefnnor acefiiilst*.

   _____ _____

h) Can you help me a moment? I can't *orst otu* who should be in which room.

   _____ _____

⑤ Summary

Read through the chapter one more time and complete the summary.

Richard Villas was working as a [1] _____ in the Grand Hotel in Valletta when he first met Elizabeth Rodgers. She was in her mid-twenties and was studying to be an [2] _____. Aurora Picardi, the manager of the hotel, told Richard it was important to make a good [3] _____ on Elizabeth because she was looking for a hotel venue for an anthropology [4] _____. Some parts of the hotel – like the conference facilities – were new, but the [5] _____ work was not finished on all the rooms.

Elizabeth had room 220 with a flat [6] _____ television, double [7] _____ and a beautiful [8] _____ of the Mediterranean from the [9] _____ .

Chapter 2

① Scanning

Read the chapter carefully. Answer these questions:

1 What is Richard looking at when Elizabeth comes into reception?
2 What does Elizabeth think of Brian?
3 What does Richard think of Brian?

② Key vocabulary

Match the words to their explanation.

1	guiltily	a	very intelligent or good at something
2	tough	b	turned brown by the sun
3	borrow	c	feel bad about something you do or have done
4	brilliant	d	to not like someone
5	imagination	e	hard and difficult
6	tanned	f	paper money
7	postpone	g	to use something belonging to another person
8	dislike	h	to move something to a later date
9	banknote	i	something that is in your head and is not real

③ Word partners

Join the word partners in the columns below together. There might be more than one possibility.

1	pick	a	age
2	by	b	a list
3	make	c	up
4	conference	d	back
5	show	e	the way
6	stone	f	minute flight
7	get	g	delegate
8	last	h	in
9	check	i	warming
10	global	j	you around

④ Practice

Read the sentences below and replace the words/phrases underlined with words and word partners from exercises 2 and 3.

a) I made later my appointment at the doctor to this afternoon.

    _____

b) It's a problem finding a hotel room in Valletta at the moment. The town is full of people attending a conference.

    _____ _____ _____

c) It's very clear that increasing temperatures on the planet is caused by car drivers.

    _____ _____

d) It's a problem having too much ability to fantasise about things. You sometimes make life too complicated.

    _____

e) What I really don't like about this job is the paperwork!

    _____

f) I've joined a tennis club. It's a really good way to make friends and keep fit.

    _____

g) Could I have €10 for a short period of time? I'll pay you back tomorrow, I promise!

    _____

h) Have you seen Karin? She's gone brown much too much on her holiday if you ask me. _____

⑤ Summary

Read through the chapter one more time and complete the summary.

Richard 1) _____ the hotel car and took Elizabeth on a tour of Malta. They visited Valletta and then had lunch at the fish market. Elizabeth talked about her 2) _____ at university, Dr Brian Butcher, who she said was very 3) _____. After lunch they went to a stone 4) _____ temple and the blue 5) _____ on the island of Commino and arrived back at the hotel in the early evening. Elizabeth was surprised to see Brian Butcher 6) _____ in at reception. He said his 7) _____ in Newcastle was 8) _____ and he took a last-minute 9) _____ to Malta to visit the hotel and Elizabeth. Richard decided he really 10) _____ Brian.

Chapter 3

① Scanning

Read the chapter carefully. Answer these questions:

1　What does Brian say about the weather in Newcastle?
2　How does Richard know about the bench where Brian and Elizabeth sit down?
3　Why does Albert telephone Brian?

② Key vocabulary

Match the words to their explanation.

1	depressed	a	reception area of a building
2	ignore	b	to say something in a sad way
3	terrible	c	down, sad
4	disinterested	d	to shine brightly
5	foyer	e	to look from one side of an area to another
6	spy	f	something illegal
7	scan	g	to pay no attention to somebody
8	bench	h	very angry
9	glitter	i	very bad
10	moan	k	a place where more than one person can sit
11	crime	l	feel neutral about something
12	interrupt	m	a statement saying you are angry about something
13	furious	n	to watch somebody without them knowing you are doing so
14	complaint	o	to stop somebody talking or doing something

③ Word partners

Join the word partners in the columns below together. There might be more than one possibility.

1	nice	a	and forwards
2	a school	b	his arm around
3	in	c	looking
4	put	d	away
5	break	e	crossed
6	backwards	f	and out
7	arms	g	of dolphins

④ Practice

Some of the words in the sentences have lost their vowels. Put them back.

a) I'm afraid we have to make a c_mpl_ _nt about the quality of the food. It's dr_ _df_l.

b) Did you see the face of the head waiter when I sent the food back? He was f_r_ _ _ s!

c) She stood there _rms cr_ss_d and _gn_r_d me for about ten minutes.

d) He's n_c_ l_ _k_ng, but not much fun. He's very d_pr_ss_d and spends the whole time m_ _ n_ ng about his job.

e) Where shall we meet? What about the hotel f_ _ _r?

⑤ Summary

Read through the chapter one more time and complete the summary.

Elizabeth and Brian had dinner together while Richard, together with Albert the head [1] _____, looked after the bar and watched them. Albert told Richard he had to do something about Brian. When his [2] _____ phone rang, Brian came out to the bar to answer it. He [3] _____ Richard and Albert and they heard him tell his wife he was in Newcastle, not in Malta. After dinner, Brian suggested he and Elizabeth should go for a walk. Richard closed the bar and went with Albert to the [4] _____ in his room on the top floor of the hotel. Using night [5] _____ they watched them walk along the sea wall to a bench with a romantic view of the sea. At that moment a school of [6] _____ swam past and Brian used the moment to put his arm around Elizabeth. He was just about to [7] _____ her when Albert phoned him and broke the atmosphere by asking what [8] _____ he would like in the morning. Elizabeth then walked back to the hotel. Brian was [9] _____ and made a [10] _____ to Richard about Albert, but Elizabeth went to her room [11] _____.

Chapter 4

① Scanning

Read the chapter carefully. Answer these questions:

1 Why does Richard go to Brian's room?
2 Where do the shutters land?
3 What does Richard break on the control console?

② Key vocabulary

Match the words to their explanation.

1	demonstration	a	physical harm to something
2	tray	b	cannot move
3	knock	c	a practical example of how something works
4	pocket	d	feeling uncomfortable or nervous about something
5	empty	e	a flat piece of wood or plastic for carrying cups etc
6	shutters	f	to shout something in a loud high voice
7	stuck	g	place in trousers or jacket where you can put money, keys etc
8	damage	h	control panel
9	embarrassed	i	empty
10	button	j	to hit a door with your hand
11	scream	k	wooden or metal covers for a window to keep out light
12	console	l	to take everything out of something
13	blank	m	something you press to turn something on or off

③ Word partners

Join the word partners in the columns below together. There might be more than one possibility.

1	take	a	in horror
2	watch	b	conferencing
3	hands	c	place
4	mess	d	on hips
5	multimedia	e	knob
6	video	f	projector
7	volume	g	down
8	turn	h	random
9	at	i	it up

④ Practice

Find the word or word partners in exercises 2 and 3 that match these descriptions.

a) How you feel if you do something stupid and your face goes red.

   _____

b) Very useful if you want to show a lot of people something on your computer.

   _____ _____

c) You turn this if you want to make the sound louder on your radio/television.

   _____ _____

d) Useful if you want to shut out the light into a room.

   _____

e) Empty, nothing there.

   _____

f) What you do if you see something that frightens you.

   _____

g) To do something without any plan or system.

   _____ _____

⑤ Summary

Read through the chapter one more time and complete the summary.

Next morning Richard went to work [1] _____. Aurora told him to take Brian his breakfast in his room. He found Brian had lost his [2] _____. Brian asked him to open the [3] _____ in the bathroom which were [4] _____. Richard pushed them too hard and to his [5] _____ they broke off the wall and fell into the hotel garden below. Luckily nobody was hurt, but Aurora told Richard he had to [6] _____ the conference equipment to Brian and Elizabeth. Richard had problems with the control panel and couldn't make it work correctly. He started the multimedia [7] _____ and the video [8] _____ equipment, but couldn't stop it, and he broke the volume [9] _____. He hit all the buttons in [10] _____ and finally stopped it. Brian was just saying how useless the hotel was when his mobile phone rang.

Chapter 5

① Scanning

Read the chapter carefully. Answer these questions:

1   Who finds Brian's passport?
2   Why does he give it to the police?
3   What do Richard and Elizabeth do together?

② Key vocabulary

Match the words to their explanation.

1	snap	a	the cause of something
2	pretend	b	sea creature with ten legs that you can eat
3	accidentally	c	to say something in an unfriendly manner
4	responsible	d	great sadness
5	chaos	e	not on purpose
6	misery	f	job or profession that you have trained for
7	daft	g	to behave in a way that is not real
8	squid	h	disorder
9	career	i	silly, stupid

③ Word partners

Join the word partners in the columns below together. There might be more than one possibility.

1	call	a	her bill
2	pour	b	with
3	deal	c	you back
4	find	d	out
5	in big	e	a flight
6	book	f	the time
7	time	g	trouble
8	pay	h	off
9	spent	i	through

④ Practice

Before Brian left Malta he received this email from his wife. Move
the underlined words in the email below to more suitable places. All
the words come from exercises 2 and 3.

To:	b.butcher@lond-uni.co.uk
From:	anne.butcher@yoohoo.com
Subject:	Why?

Dear Brian,
Don't a) **responsible** that you went to Malta on business. You were with someone,
weren't you? One of your students I expect. I just don't trust you these days.
I feel really b) **career** and you are completely c) **bill**. I can't go out anywhere
because I am so upset. The house is in d) **trouble**. You are in big e) **miserable** when
I see you.
I am going to Majorca for a holiday. My f) **chaos** is tomorrow. I paid the g) **pretend**
with your credit card. You can have two weeks to think about your actions. I don't
care about your h) **flight** any more. We'll talk about our future when I come back.
Anne

a) _____ b) _____ c) _____ d) _____
e) _____ f) _____ g) _____ h) _____

⑤ Summary

Read through the chapter one more time and complete the summary.

Brian's wife found out that Brian was in Malta, not Newcastle, and she was very
1) _____ with him. Albert was 2) _____. He found Brian's passport
on the bench by the sea wall and took it to the 3) _____ station and they
called his wife in England and told her that Brian was in Malta, not Newcastle
as she thought. He was, of course, in 4) _____ trouble and booked a
5) _____ back to England that night.

Elizabeth stayed on for two more days and Richard had some
6) _____ off so he could 7) _____ it with her. They did a lot of things
together and at the end of the time Richard decided he would go back to
London and try to find a 8) _____ job and have a proper 9) _____
and not just stay a barman in Malta. As Albert said, the most important thing
was for him to follow Elizabeth.

FISH LEGS – EXERCISES

Chapter 1

① Scanning

Read the chapter carefully. Answer these questions:

1 How do Richard and Elizabeth travel to Kiyoyama?
2 Is the hotel always empty?
3 What do the people in Kiyoyama do for a living?

② Key vocabulary

Match the words to their explanation.

1	tip	a	in good physical condition
2	custard	b	behaving with good manners
3	absurd	c	the end of something, especially something pointed
4	healthy	d	passage connecting rooms
5	stuff	e	to make somebody ill with food or drink
6	politely	f	vanilla sauce
7	corridor	g	plant that grows in the sea
8	chambermaid	h	stupid and ridiculous
9	poison	i	woman who cleans rooms in a hotel
10	seaweed	j	substance

③ Word partners

Join the word partners in the columns below together. There might be more than one possibility.

1	the end	a	board
2	past their	b	a room
3	book	c	of the table
4	shake	d	set
5	half	e	from
6	ghost	f	sell-by date
7	sun	g	hotel
8	apart	h	his head

④ Practice

Put the words in the following sentences into the correct order so that they make sense. The first word is correct.

a) Food its healthy sell by past date isn't.

_____

b) I a tip gave chambermaid the.

_____

c) We board for three booked half nights.

_____

d) Apart toothbrush stuff other from didn't my bring I any.

_____

e) I end the passport my left of on the table.

_____

⑤ Summary

Read through the chapter one more time and complete the summary.

Richard Villas and Elizabeth Rodgers [1] _____ a room in a hotel in a small [2] _____ village in Japan. Other foreigners at work said they should learn about the real Japan in the countryside because Tokyo was too [3] _____, so they travelled by train and bus to Kiyoyama, 100 kilometres outside Tokyo. Their first difficulty was that the [4] _____ could not understand their names, but the hotel manager, Mr Segiguchi, spoke very good English because he had worked in London. Mr Segiguchi explained the hotel was [5] _____ at the moment but that a big [6] _____ party would come at the weekend. He showed them their traditional Japanese bedroom with a [7] _____ floor and a *futon* for a bed, and told them that the [8] _____ would bring them a dinner with many Japanese [9] _____ to their room in the evening.

Chapter 2

① Scanning

Read the chapter carefully. Answer these questions:

1 What does Mr Segiguchi show Richard?
2 How many people sit in the wooden bath tubs?
3 What do Elizabeth and Richard do after lunch?

② Key vocabulary

Match the words to their explanation.

1	rude	a	something which controls water in a bath
2	lie	b	to do something with another person
3	tap	c	not polite
4	traditional	d	to have something happen to you
5	share	e	to massage
6	experience	f	more good fortune
7	rub	g	something that has been happening for many years
8	luckier	h	to say things which are untrue

③ Word partners

Join the word partners in the columns below together. There might be more than one possibility.

1	from time	a	it back
2	cross-	b	into
3	send	c	to time
4	powerful	d	a corner
5	rubbish	e	smell
6	turn	f	legged
7	bump	g	feature
8	special	h	bin

③ Practice

Read the sentences below and replace the underlined words/phrases with something suitable from exercises 2 and 3.

a) Taste <u>modern</u> French cuisine at 'Les Pantoffles' – Rue St Jacques 27.

   _____

b) The problem with politicians is that they often <u>tell the truth</u>.

   _____

c) I <u>missed seeing</u> an old friend at the conference.

   _____ _____

d) We phone each other <u>every day</u>.

   _____ _____ ____ _____

e) I don't like this shop. The staff are so <u>polite</u>.

   _____

f) The underwater restaurant is a <u>standard</u> feature of our hotel.

   _____

⑤ Summary

Read through the chapter one more time and complete the summary.

Richard and Elizabeth didn't like their Japanese dinner, but because it was
1) _____ to send it back they put it in a plastic bag to
2) _____ away in a 3) _____ bin. Richard however
4) _____ into Mr Segiguchi in the corridor, who asked if he could help
him. Richard lied and said he wanted to see the *sento* – which were a special
5) _____ of the hotel. Mr Segiguchi showed him and explained how
visitors had to share the 6) _____ bath tub with other people. He
promised to bring him on Friday night when it was open.

   Next day Elizabeth and Richard threw away the breakfast – some of which
looked like fish legs in 7) _____ – and went to visit the
8) _____ and then 9) _____ in the sea. They had lunch in
the single restaurant in Kiyoyama and then went for a 10) _____
in the hotel.

Chapter 3

① Scanning

Read the chapter carefully. Answer these questions:

1   What are the hotel staff doing?
2   What does Mr Segiguchi find Richard doing?
3   Why is Richard embarrassed?

② Key vocabulary

Match the words to their explanation.

1	shake	a	move with difficulty, not flexible
2	sunburnt	b	to move your head up and down to show agreement
3	hairdryer	c	to hold something and move it backwards and forwards very fast
4	lobster	d	something that tastes very good
5	delicious	e	very sad
6	stiff	f	when the skin goes red after being out in the sun too long
7	horrible	g	electrical device for drying hair
8	upset	h	sea animal with legs, that goes red when cooked
9	nod	i	extremely bad

③ Word partners

Join the word partners in the columns below together. There might be more than one possibility.

1	win	a	as possible
2	as little	b	cleaning
3	to hunt	c	an argument
4	come	d	the house
5	vacuum	e	off
6	trip	f	in
7	a telling	g	to life
8	joined	h	over
9	on	i	down

④ Practice

The letters in the words and word partners in italics are in alphabetical order. Rewrite them so they make sense. They are all from exercises 2 and 3.

Charlotte: This is my favourite seafood restaurant. Have you tried the a) *belorst* yet?

Natasha: No, but I will; it looks b) *cdeiilous*! By the way, have you heard about Anne and Brian?

Charlotte: Yes, I spoke to Anne this morning. She said she was really c) *epstu* when the police phoned from Malta!

Natasha: I know, I was there! She called Brian on his mobile immediately and gave him a good d) *egillnt ffo*. He pretended he was in Newcastle!

Charlotte: Well, he could never e) *inw* that *aegmnrtu*. Does she know what he was doing?

Natasha: She thinks he was chasing after some student of his, f) *behilorr* man!

Charlotte: Yes, he's awful. He does as little as g) *beilopss* at home and goes out the whole time …

a _____   b _____   c _____   d _____

e _____   f _____   g _____

⑤ Summary

Read through the chapter one more time and complete the summary.

When he woke from his siesta, Richard found he was badly [1] _____.
Elizabeth told him that when she went to ask at reception for a [2] _____
she could smell the dinner they had thrown away. She said if they didn't get it
back the [3] _____ would find it and know it was from them. Richard set
off to [4] _____ it down but Mr Segiguchi picked up the bag when Richard
[5] _____ over the rubbish bin. Richard explained that they didn't like the
food. Mr Segiguchi was [6] _____ and went to bring the [7] _____
to their room. Elizabeth and Richard expected a [8] _____ off but he just
asked them what they would like to eat so he could prepare it. Then Mr
Segiguchi told them to go to the bar and have a drink on the [9] _____.

Chapter 4

① Scanning

Read the chapter carefully. Answer these questions:

1 What do Richard and Elizabeth eat for breakfast?
2 What do the other guests wear around the hotel?
3 What happens when Elizabeth and Richard enter the bar?

② Key vocabulary

Match the words to their explanation.

1	wander	a	bright lights used on a stage to light up the performers
2	reduce	b	place where a show takes place
3	tender	c	to walk around with no clear direction
4	shy	d	to show how much you like a performance usually by clapping hands together
5	stage	e	to take hold of something quickly and hold it hard
6	transform	f	to make smaller
7	applaud	g	sensitive
8	spotlights	h	to change
9	grab	i	nervous and embarrassed about talking to strangers

③ Word partners

Join the word partners in the columns below together. There might be more than one possibility.

1	cries	a	tight together
2	coach	b	end of the …
3	surface	c	of delight
4	pack	d	of drums
5	chocolates	e	heels
6	loud	f	differences
7	at the	g	costumes
8	a roll	h	load
9	high	i	in a box
10	sparkling	j	speaker

④ Practice

Choose vocabulary items or word partners from exercises 2 and 3 to complete the sentences below.

a) The speaker stood on the _____ and spoke for about half an hour.

b) The whole of the centre of town is full of _____ _____ of tourists from Germany.

c) If we want this project to work we must focus on the similarities not the _____ _____ between Americans and Europeans.

d) My feet are killing me. I shouldn't wear _____ _____ all day.

e) When the speaker finished her talk everybody _____ loudly.

f) My boss asked if I wanted to meet the CEO of the company, but I said no. I was too _____.

g) I couldn't hear her presentation at all. The _____ _____ weren't working and I was too far away.

⑤ Summary

Read through the chapter one more time and complete the summary.

In the bar Richard and Elizabeth met six Filipino women who would be doing the cabaret on the next evening. They promised they would come to see the show and after their drink went back to their room and had a [1] _____ dinner.

On Friday morning they saw three [2] _____ loads of hotel guests arriving from Tokyo for the weekend. Mr Segiguchi spent a lot of time [3] _____ and organising them as they got out and went off to their rooms to change into *yukata* and then [4] _____ around the hotel and the village.

In the evening Mr Segiguchi took them to the *sento*. Richard and Mr Segiguchi sat together with two other men in the bath tub and Richard had to answer lots of questions from all the other guests. Then they went to the bar to see the [5] _____. As soon as they came in they were asked to join a table and given food and drink and then the cabaret started. The cabaret girls looked completely different in their [6] _____ heels and sparkling [7] _____. The guests [8] _____ everything enthusiastically. Then Esmeralda, the leader of the group, asked for people to come on stage to join them and the [9] _____ started searching for Elizabeth and Richard.

Chapter 5

① Scanning

Read the chapter carefully. Answer these questions:

1 What do Richard and Elizabeth have to wear on stage?
2 What kind of music do they dance to?
3 What does Richard learn about Japan?

② Key vocabulary

Match the words to their explanation.

1	maracas	a	to hit both hands together to show you like something
2	imitate	b	people who watch a show or performance
3	whisper	c	pair of hollow balls with little stones inside used for music
4	clap	d	a bad headache usually after drinking too much
5	hysterically	e	the taste of something horrible or unpleasant
6	audience	f	to copy
7	hangover	g	to give something
8	disgusting	h	to speak in a low quiet voice
9	contribute	i	out of control

③ Word partners

Join the word partners in the columns below together. There might be more than one possibility.

1	swing	a	of applause
2	in time	b	voice
3	side	c	their hips
4	a round	d	a turn
5	stand	e	to side
6	have	f	off
7	take	g	in line
8	a weak	h	to the beat

④ Practice

Elizabeth wrote an email to her mother. Move the words in bold in the email below to more suitable places. All the words come from exercises 2 and 3.

To: janette21@hitmail.com
From: e.rodgers@yoohoo.com
Subject: Mini-break

Dear Mum,
Richard and I went for a short holiday outside Tokyo. What an interesting hotel! Last night we went to the cabaret and the a) **hangover** made us join the cabaret performers on stage. We had to b) **taking** them – a sort of c) **beat** to side d) **turn** swinging, Hawaiian style dancing, not easy to do in time to the e) **side**!) and then afterwards Richard spent half the evening singing karaoke while all the men in the audience wanted to have a f) **hip** dancing with me!
Richard had a little too much to drink and fell asleep before I even finished g) **imitate** off my makeup. Next morning of course he had a terrible h) **audience** but then …

a) _____ b) _____ c) _____ d) _____
e) _____ f) _____ g) _____ h) _____

⑤ Summary

Read through the chapter one more time and complete the summary.

Elizabeth and Richard had to dance a 1) _____ dance with the cabaret girls on the 2) _____. The audience 3) _____ and laughed 4) _____ and afterwards gave them a big round of 5) _____. For the rest of the evening they drank with the guests and the company executives all stood in 6) _____ to dance with Elizabeth. Richard sang 'Yellow Submarine' with the 7) _____ machine five times until finally Elizabeth took the 8) _____ away from him and took him back to their bedroom.

The next morning he had a bad hangover, but Mr Segiguchi gave him a drink which tasted 9) _____ but helped. Richard thought about his holiday. He had learnt that the real Japan was not just about temples and traditional Japanese food. The real Japan was about being happy to 10) _____ something to the group.

BROOKE'S HOTEL – EXERCISES

Chapter 1

1 Scanning

Read the chapter carefully. Answer these questions:

1   Why is Elizabeth flying to Kuching?
2   Who does Richard work for?
3   How do Elizabeth and Richard travel to Brooke's Hotel from the airport?

2 Key vocabulary

Match the words to their explanation.

1	pre-book	a	very afraid
2	critic	b	a drug to make somebody calm and quiet
3	advertising	c	change in advance
4	cockroach	d	woollen cloth to keep you warm in bed
5	rational	e	somebody whose job is to judge good and bad qualities of books, films etc.
6	terrified	f	to look bright
7	tranquillizer	g	the business of telling people about products so they buy them
8	grant	h	brown/black insect which usually lives in buildings, especially in warmer countries
9	blanket	i	sensible, something based on reason
10	shine	j	a sum of money from an organisation

3 Word partners

Join the word partners in the columns below together. There might be more than one possibility.

1	advertising	a	proof
2	run	b	off
3	business	c	agency
4	good	d	heat
5	air	e	trip
6	tropical	f	to another
7	bullet	g	conditioned
8	set	h	away
9	one	i	discount

④ Practice

The letters in the words and word partners in italics are in alphabetical order. Rewrite them so they make sense. They are all from exercises 2 and 3.

a) The whole department is *deefiirrt* of the possibility of job cuts.

_____

b) He applied for a *agnrt* to study in Belorussia.

_____

c) Did you know Richard Villas worked in *adegiinrstv* before he became a famous author?

_____

d) After the accident the doctor gave me a *aeiillnrrtuqz* to calm me down.

_____

e) I'm not buying this unless you give me a *dgoo cdinostu*.

_____ _____

f) The staff were whispering to one *aehnort* about me as I came in to the office.

_____

g) I've just bought the latest novel from Richard Villas. The *cciirts* say it's really good.

_____

⑤ Summary

Read through the chapter one more time and complete the summary.

Richard and Elizabeth Villas arrived in Kuching, Malaysia and went to stay at Brooke's Hotel. They were there because Elizabeth had an [1] _____ at the anthropology [2] _____ of the university. She hoped to get a three year [3] _____ to study a [4] _____ _____ tribe on the island called the Kokketti. There would be enough money for Richard to give up his job at an [5] _____ agency and finish his second novel. They would live in a house on the university [6] _____ in Kuching

But there was a problem; Richard was terrified of [7] _____ and so they needed to stay in a good hotel where they hoped there would not be too many. They didn't have very much money so they were pleased to get a good [8] _____ on the price of the room.

Chapter 2

① Scanning

Read the chapter carefully. Answer these questions:

1 Are Richard and Elizabeth married?
2 What is *durian*?
3 What was the slogan Richard wrote for Love Cola?

② Key vocabulary

Match the words to their explanation.

1	headquarters	a	area of well-cut grass in a garden
2	polished	b	dark strong wood used sometimes for furniture
3	reflect	c	main office of a company
4	squeak	d	a short phrase that is easy to remember, used for advertising
5	courtyard	e	money you pay every month for a flat, apartment or house
6	mahogany	f	to rub something to make it shiny
7	lawn	g	plants in a group
8	clump	h	to mirror something
9	rent	i	to make a high noise, like a mouse
10	slogan	j	central area in a building which is uncovered and open to the outside

③ Word partners

Join the word partners in the columns below together. There might be more than one possibility.

1	colonial	a	the years
2	turn	b	and dark
3	over	c	building
4	guide	d	wet weather
5	cool	e	forms
6	bright	f	book
7	registration	g	(his) time
8	cold	h	sunshine
9	great	i	into
10	wasting	j	future

④ Practice

Read the sentences below and replace the underlined words/phrases with something more suitable from exercises 2 and 3.

a) What I love about Italy is the <u>cold, wet weather</u>.

_____ _____

b) All the important company decisions are made at the <u>branch office</u>.

_____

c) London is so expensive. We can only afford to <u>buy</u> a house.

_____

d) Roberto is <u>using</u> his <u>time well</u> working here. He just isn't up to the job.

_____ _____ _____

e) A <u>terrible past</u> is what you get when you work in the microelectronics field.

_____ _____

f) What we need for Love Cola is a great <u>long description</u>. Something like 'Open Love. Love life!'

_____

⑤ Summary

Read through the chapter one more time and complete the summary.

Brooke's Hotel was a [1] _____ building which had been the [2] _____ of a 19th century [3] _____ company and had become a hotel in the 1920s. Many [4] _____ people had stayed there. It was old [5] -_____ and traditional with dark [6] _____ floors and chandeliers. They took the lift to the second floor and Richard saw his first cockroach in the [7] _____. However he said nothing to Elizabeth and they got to their room which was very beautiful with a view of the green [8] _____ and clumps of [9] _____ in the hotel gardens.

That evening they went to the food [10] _____ and had a perfect evening with warm weather, good food and friendly people. They both thought it would be wonderful to live there rather than in cold grey London.

Chapter 3

① Scanning

Read the chapter carefully. Answer these questions:

1　Why is *Roacherize* illegal?
2　Does it kill all the cockroaches?
3　Why does Richard want to talk to the chef?

② Key vocabulary

Match the words to their explanation.

1	steady	a	sound made by something hard or rough
2	illegal	b	feeling very afraid
3	effective	c	regular, continuous, without stopping
4	spray	d	to collect stuff on the floor together with a brush
5	scratching	e	produces good results
6	panic	f	not allowed by law
7	fold	g	to help somebody remember something
8	attract	h	to go over an area and find out what is there
9	sweep	i	to cover something with a thin layer of liquid
10	explore	j	to make someone/something interested in something
11	remind	k	to bend a piece of paper in half

③ Word partners

Join the word partners in the columns below together. There might be more than one possibility.

1	brushed	a	down
2	insect	b	and dustpan
3	just	c	their teeth
4	lay	d	hunters
5	in	e	in case
6	a brush	f	bracelet
7	head	g	despair
8	ivory	h	spray

④ Practice

Some of the words in the sentences have lost their vowels.
Put them back.

a) The company gave the President of Kazbakistan an expensive present. This was of course _ll_g_l.

b) The chemicals from the _ns_ct spr_y were p_ _s_n_ _s and some people and animals died.

c) You'd better bring your credit card, j_st _n c_s_ we run out of money.

d) Share prices on the stock market dropped by 50% due to p_n_c selling. Traders were _n d_sp_ _r as companies worldwide lost $2 trillion.

e) The crisis r_m_nd_d everybody of the Wall Street crash of 1929.

f) We need to _xpl_r_ ways to _ttr_ct more investment for the company.

g) She f_ld_d the letter and put it into the envelope.

⑤ Summary

Read through the chapter one more time and complete the summary.

After Elizabeth was asleep that night, Richard [1) _____ their bathroom with an insect 2) _____ called *Roacherize*, which was extremely 3) _____, to make sure he had no problems with cockroaches. But two hours later he heard a 4) _____ noise from the bathroom and when he looked inside he saw hundreds of dead and dying cockroaches lying on their backs. He 5) _____ them up and threw out of the window, but to his horror he saw a very large cockroach looking at him through the window.

The next day Elizabeth went shopping and Richard 6) _____ the hotel, which was similar to a 7) _____ with old pictures, books and even weapons from the times of the head 8) _____. When Elizabeth came back they went to have lunch in the hotel restaurant. Richard was disappointed with the menu, which had a lot of old 9) _____ English food. Richard decided to interview the chef as he could be good 10) _____ for Richard's novel.

Chapter 4

① Scanning

Read the chapter carefully. Answer these questions:

1 What language is Elizabeth studying?
2 What three weapons does Richard use on the cockroach?
3 Why can't Richard and Elizabeth eat dinner in the hotel restaurant that night?

② Key vocabulary

Match the words to their explanation.

1	nectar	a	to speak with somebody and ask them questions
2	determined	b	very pleased with
3	refrigerator	c	sweet liquid in plants
4	pile	d	so loud you cannot hear anything anymore
5	interview	e	a strong wish to do something
6	blow	f	a person who does something illegal
7	proud	g	to place one on top of another
8	deafening	h	electrical device to keep food or drink cold
9	incredible	i	fall from side to side
10	stagger	j	a hard hit
11	criminal	k	difficult to believe

③ Word partners

Join the word partners in the columns below together. There might be more than one possibility.

1	ready	a	zero
2	ground	b	herself
3	frying	c	for action
4	proud	d	on
5	throw	e	asleep
6	hot	f	of
7	fast	g	spicy sauce
8	rub	h	pan
9	insist	i	her eyes

④ Practice

Choose vocabulary items or word partners from exercises 2 and 3 to complete the sentences below.

a) Nuraan isn't happy in her current work. So she had an _____ today at another company for another job.

b) The company dress code is very strict. They _____ _____ men wearing ties and women wearing skirts.

c) The first quarter results show an _____ 90% increase in profits for the company.

d) There was so much noise in the canteen we couldn't think. It was _____!

e) Poor Hiro was so tired this morning after last night that he fell _____ at his desk. His boss fired him.

f) Jean-Paul may go to prison. His share dealings were _____.

⑤ Summary

Read through the chapter one more time and complete the summary.

Richard went to the hotel kitchen to 1) _____ for the chef, but found nobody was there. He was just about to go when he saw the large cockroach that he had seen twice before. He hit her with a 2) _____ pan but also hit a pile of 3) _____ and glasses on a table. Unfortunately he didn't even manage to 4) _____ the cockroach. She jumped up and 5) _____ across the kitchen and landed on the wall above the door. Richard threw a bottle of chilli sauce which 6) _____ on the wall, just as the chef came in and was hit in the face by the sauce. Richard 7) _____ before the chef saw who he was.

Richard came back to the hotel after having a 8) _____ and buying new clothes, and found Elizabeth fast asleep. She had to agree to go outside of the hotel for dinner but 9) _____ on taking a taxi. Richard thought it was because she was 10) _____ about him seeing a cockroach.

Chapter 5

① Scanning

Read the chapter carefully. Answer these questions:

1 Who does Richard talk to about football?
2 Why does Richard want to leave Kuching?
3 Why does Elizabeth want to leave Kuching?

② Key vocabulary

Match the words to their explanation.

1	chase	a	something that annoys you and gets on your nerves
2	breathe	b	to cry
3	mumble	c	to run after something and try and catch it
4	fake	d	short thick finger on your hand
5	dislike	e	flattened
6	irritating	f	to treat somebody or something as a god or goddess
7	sip	g	to take in air
8	pant	h	to breathe very quickly especially after some exercise
9	sob	i	not liking somebody
10	worship	j	not real
11	thumb	k	to drink a small amount from a glass or bottle
12	squashed	l	to talk in a way which is difficult to understand

③ Word partners

Join the word partners in the columns below together. There might be more than one possibility.

1	half	a	shut
2	took	b	your mind
3	on	c	dressed
4	at peace	d	display
5	slam	e	bear
6	on	f	beginning to end
7	change	g	his mind off
8	burst	h	the edge of
9	can't	i	with the world
10	from	j	into tears

④ Practice

Elizabeth wrote an email to her boss Hilary in London. Move the words in bold in the email below to more suitable places. All the words come from exercises 2 and 3.

To: h.niblock@lond-uni.co.uk
From: e.villas@yoohoo.com
Subject: Mini-break

Dear Hilary,
You will be pleased to know that I have changed my a) **chasing** about wanting to work at the University of Kuching. I found out today that the Kokketti b) **bear** rats and as you know I c) **fake** rats intensely. And in a stone-age village I won't be able to take my mind d) **dislike** the problem by shopping. Anyway, as you know Richard can't e) **worship** cockroaches, and he had an enormous one f) **mind** him (I finally killed it with a book) so it would not have been possible for him to stay.
So, we're coming back next week. Would you like me to buy you something? They have really incredible g) **off** Cartier and Patek watches in the markets. Let me know and see you soon.
Love,
Elizabeth

a) _____ b) _____ c) _____ d) _____
e) _____ f) _____ g) _____

⑤ Summary

Read through the chapter one more time and complete the summary.

The next day Elizabeth went for her interview at the university and Richard took his 1) _____ off his troubles by exploring Kuching. He enjoyed himself a lot and after a good meal went back to the hotel to sit on his 2) _____ and wait for Elizabeth. He opened a bottle of Love Cola, sat back – and saw the large cockroach from the kitchen on the 3) _____ of the balcony, just before she 4) _____ onto his chair. He decided he couldn't stay in Kuching and as he had a shower thought how he could tell Elizabeth.

When he came out of the shower he found Elizabeth waiting for him on the 5) _____ of the bed. She had been 6) _____ the grant by the university but she too didn't want to stay in Kuching. She had found out that the Kokketti tribespeople 7) _____ rats, which she couldn't 8) _____. And all the time when Richard had been seeing cockroaches she had been seeing rats. Richard told her about his problems and Elizabeth showed him the 9) _____ of the book, *Kokketti for Beginners*, which she had used to 10) _____ his enemy.

ANSWERS
Room Service

Chapter 1

Skim questions

The Grand Hotel is in Valletta, Malta

He works as a barman, receptionist, waiter, bellboy and so on.

It's more than a hundred years old.

1 Scan questions

    1 Elizabeth studies anthropology.

    2 Elizabeth wants to see if it would be suitable for a conference.

    3 The head porter is called Albert Cini.

2 Key vocabulary

    1 – c 2 – f 3 – a 4 – j 5 – h 6 – b 7 – e 8 – d 9 – i 10 – g

3 Word partners

    1 – c 2 – j / b 3 – f 4 – i 5 – a / g 6 – g 7 – d / h 8 – b / e / f 9 – h

    10 – e / f

4 Practice

    a – on average b – impress c – installed d – suitable e – fall off

    f – tip / change g – sort out

5 Summary

    1 – bellboy 2 – anthropologist 3 – impression 4 – conference

    5 – restoration 6 – screen 7 – bed 8 – view 9 – balcony

Chapter 2

Skim questions

Richard shows Elizabeth all over Malta.

Brian Butcher is Elizabeth's university tutor.

Brian decides to come to see the Grand Hotel – and Elizabeth!

1 Scan questions

    1 Richard is looking through Elizabeth's passport.

    2 Elizabeth clearly likes Brian a lot.

    3 Richard doesn't like Brian.

2 Key vocabulary

    1 – c 2 – e 3 – g 4 – a 5 – i 6 – b 7 – h 8 – d 9 – f

3 Word partners

    1 – c 2 – e 3 – b 4 – g 5 – j / c / e 6 – a 7 – d 8 – f 9 – h / d 10 – i

4 Practice

    a – postponed b – conference delegates c – global warming d – imagination

    e – dislike f – brilliant g – borrow h – tanned

5 Summary

    1 – borrowed 2 – tutor 3 – brilliant 4 – age 5 – lagoon 6 – checking

    7 – seminar 8 – postponed 9 – flight 10 – disliked

Chapter 3

Skim questions

Brian's wife thinks he is in Newcastle.

Brian and Elizabeth go for a walk along the sea wall.

Brian complains about Albert because his phone call interrupted him.

1 Scan questions

1   Brian says the weather is very bad in Newcastle.

2   Richard has sat on the bench with a girl in the past.

3   Albert phones Brian to interrupt him kissing Elizabeth.

2 Key vocabulary

1 – c   2 – g   3 – i   4 – l   5 – a   6 – n   7 – e   8 – k   9 – d   10 – b

11 – f   12 – o   13 – h   14 – m

3 Word partners

1 – c   2 – g   3 – f   4 – b / d   5 – d   6 – a   7 – a

4 Practice

a – complaint / dreadful   b – furious   c – arms crossed / ignored

d – nice looking / depressed / moaning

5 Summary

1 – porter   2 – mobile   3 – ignored   4 – balcony   5 – binoculars / glasses

6 – dolphins   7 – kiss   8 – newspaper   9 – furious   10 – complaint

11 – alone

Chapter 4

Skim questions

Brian has lost his passport.

Richard breaks the shutters in the bathroom by accident.

Richard doesn't know how to operate it.

1 Scan questions

1   Richard takes Brian his breakfast.

2   The shutters land in the hotel garden.

3   Richard breaks the volume knob.

2 Key vocabulary

1 – c   2 – e   3 – j   4 – g   5 – l   6 – k   7 – b   8 – a   9 – d   10 – m

11 – f   12 – h   13 – i

3 Word partners

1 – c   2 – a   3 – d / g   4 – i   5 – f   6 – b / f   7 – e   8 – i / g   9 – a / h

4 Practice

a – embarrassed   b – multimedia projector   c – volume knob   d – shutters

e – blank   f – scream   g – at random

5 Summary

1 – early   2 – passport   3 – shutters   4 – stuck   5 – horror

6 – demonstrate   7 – projector   8 – conferencing   9 – knob   10 – panic

Chapter 5

Skim questions

Brian's wife calls because the police called her to say they had found Brian's passport.
The conference won't take place in Malta.
He wants to follow Elizabeth and get a job.

1 Scan questions

1 Albert finds Brian's passport on the bench.
2 Albert gives it to the police because he doesn't like Brian.
3 Richard and Elizabeth swim, go fishing and go to lots of bars and restaurants.

2 Key vocabulary

1 – c   2 – g   3 – e   4 – a   5 – h   6 – d   7 – i   8 – b   9 – f

3 Word partners

1 – c   2 – i / d   3 – b   4 – d / e / f   5 – g   6 – e / b   7 – h / d   8 – a / b / c / d
9 – b / f

4 Practice

a – pretend   b – miserable   c – responsible   d – chaos   e – trouble
f – flight   g – bill   h - career

5 Summary

1 – angry   2 – responsible   3 – police   4 – big   5 – flight   6 – time
7 – spend   8 – sensible   9 – career

Fish Legs

Chapter 1

Skim questions

Richard and Elizabeth don't like their breakfast.

They arrive at the hotel on Wednesday afternoon.

Mr Segiguchi speaks good English because he worked in London.

1 Scan questions

1 Richard and Elizabeth travel to Kiyoyama by train and bus.

2 The hotel is not empty at the weekends.

3 Mostly they are fisherpeople.

2 Key vocabulary

1 – c   2 – f   3 – h   4 – a   5 – j   6 – b   7 – d   8 – i   9 – e   10 – g

3 Word partners

1 – c   2 – f   3 – b   4 – h   5 – a   6 – g   7 – d   8 – e

4 Practice

a   Food past its sell by date isn't healthy.

b   I gave the chambermaid a tip.

c   We booked half board for three nights.

d   Apart from my toothbrush I didn't bring any other stuff.

e   I left my passport on the end of the table.

5 Summary

1 – booked   2 – fishing   3 – westernized   4 – receptionist   5 – empty

6 – office   7 – tatami   8 – chambermaid   9 – specialities

Chapter 2

Skim questions

Richard and Elizabeth eat their dinner sitting on the *tatami* in their hotel room.

They put the dinner in a plastic bag and throw it away in a rubbish bin.

They go to have a look at the temple in the village and then go swimming.

1 Scan questions

1 Mr Segiguchi shows Richard the *sento* in the hotel.

2 Four people sit in each bath tub.

3 Elizabeth and Richard go to have a siesta.

2 Key vocabulary

1 – c   2 – h   3 – a   4 – g   5 – b   6 – d   7 – e   8 – f

3 Word partners

1 – c   2 – f   3 – a   4 – e   5 – h   6 – a / d   7 – b   8 – e / g

4 Practice

a – traditional   b – lie   c – bumped into   d – from time to time   e – rude

f – special

5 Summary

1 – rude   2 – throw   3 – rubbish   4 – bumped   5 – feature   6 – wooden

7 – custard   8 – temple   9 – swam   10 – siesta

Chapter 3

Skim questions

Richard didn't put on any suntan cream.

The smell is caused by the dinner Richard threw away in the rubbish bin.

The chef wants to find out what Richard and Elizabeth would like to eat for dinner.

1 Scan questions

  1 The hotel staff are getting the rooms ready for the weekend guests.

  2 Mr Segiguchi finds Richard with his hand in the rubbish bin.

  3 Richard is embarrassed because he and Elizabeth have upset Mr Segiguchi.

2 Key vocabulary

  1 – c 2 – f 3 – g 4 – h 5 – d 6 – a 7 – i 8 – e 9 – b

3 Word partners

  1 – c 2 – a 3 – i 4 – g 5 – b 6 – h 7 – e 8 – f 9 – d

4 Practice

  a – lobster b – delicious c – upset d – telling off e – win that argument

  f – horrible g – possible

5 Summary

  1 – sunburnt 2 – hairdryer 3 – staff 4 – hunt 5 – tripped 6 – upset

  7 – chef 8 – telling 9 – house

Chapter 4

Skim questions

They are the cabaret dancers.

The new guests are all from one company in Tokyo.

They enjoy the *sento* but didn't find it very relaxing.

1 Scan questions

  1 Elizabeth and Richard have coffee, cornflakes, eggs and toast for breakfast.

  2 The other guests wear *yukata*.

  3 When they enter the bar, the other guests make them sit at a table near the stage.

2 Key vocabulary

  1 – c 2 – f 3 – g 4 – i 5 – b 6 – h 7 – d 8 – a 9 – e

3 Word partners

  1 – c 2 – h 3 – f 4 – a 5 – i 6 – j 7 – b 8 – d 9 – e 10 – g

4 Practice

  a – stage b – coach loads c – surface differences d – high heels

  e – applauded f – shy g - loudspeakers.

5 Summary

  1 – delicious 2 – coach 3 – bowing 4 – wandered 5 – cabaret

  6 – high 7 – costumes 8 – applauded / clapped 9 – spotlights

Chapter 5

Skim questions

Elizabeth and Richard have to dance with the cabaret girls.

He sings 'Yellow Submarine'.

Yes, they do enjoy their holiday.

1 Scan questions

1 They have to wear grass skirts, a grassy bikini top (Elizabeth) and a flowery necklace (Richard).

2 They dance to Hawaiian style music.

3 Richard learns that the important thing is to contribute something to the group, even if it isn't very good.

2 Key vocabulary

1 – c   2 – f   3 – h   4 – a   5 – i   6 – b   7 – d   8 – e   9 – g

3 Word partners

1 – c   2 – h   3 – e   4 – a   5 – g   6 – d   7 – f   8 – b

4 Practice

a – audience   b – imitate   c – side   d – hip   e – beat   f – turn   g – taking

h - hangover

5 Summary

1 – Hawaiian   2 – stage   3 – clapped   4 – hysterically   5 – applause

6 – line   7 – karaoke   8 – microphone   9 – disgusting   10 – contribute

Brooke's Hotel

Chapter 1

Skim questions
Elizabeth and Richard have landed in Kuching on the island of Borneo.
Richard is terrified of cockroaches.
They choose Brooke's Hotel.

1 Scan questions
1 Elizabeth has an interview at the anthropology department of the university in Kuching.
2 Richard works for an advertising agency.
3 They travel to the hotel in the airport bus.

2 Key vocabulary
1 – c 2 – e 3 – g 4 – h 5 – i 6 – a 7 – b 8 – j 9 – d 10 – f

3 Word partners
1 – c 2 – h 3 – e 4 – i 5 – g 6 – d 7 – a 8 – b 9 – f

4 Practice
a – terrified b – grant c – advertising d – tranquillizer e – good discount
f – another g - critics

5 Summary
1 – interview 2 – department 3 – grant 4 – stone age 5 – advertising
6 – campus 7 – cockroaches 8 – discount

Chapter 2

Skim questions
Brooke's Hotel was the headquarters for the Borneo Trading Company Ltd in the 19th century.
Richard sees a cockroach.
They eat supper in the food stalls.

1 Scan questions
1 Richard and Elizabeth are married.
2 *Durian* is a kind of fruit.
3 Richard's slogan was 'Open Love! Love life!'.

2 Key vocabulary
1 – c 2 – f 3 – h 4 – i 5 – j 6 – b 7 – a 8 – g 9 – e 10 – d

3 Word partners
1 – c 2 – i 3 – a 4 – f 5 – b 6 – h 7 – e 8 – d 9 – j 10 – g

4 Practice
a – bright sunshine b – headquarters c – rent d – wasting his time
e – great future f – slogan

5 Summary
1 – colonial 2 – headquarters 3 – trading 4 – famous 5 – fashioned
6 – mahogany 7 – corridor 8 – lawns 9 – bamboos 10 – stalls

Chapter 3

Skim questions

Richard sprays *Roacherize* around the bathroom.

Charles Brooke was the second White Rajah of Sarawak.

Richard is disappointed by the restaurant.

1 Scan questions

1 *Roacherize* is very poisonous.

2 No. One very large cockroach isn't killed.

3 Richard wants to talk to the chef because he thinks he might have some interesting stories for his novel.

2 Key vocabulary

1 – c   2 – f   3 – e   4 – i   5 – a   6 – b   7 – k   8 – j   9 – d   10 – h

11 – g

3 Word partners

1 – c   2 – h   3 – e   4 – a   5 – g   6 – b   7 – d   8 – f

4 Practice

a – illegal   b – insect spray / poisonous   c – just in case   d – panic

e – reminded   f – explore / attract   g - folded

5 Summary

1 – sprayed   2 – spray   3 – poisonous   4 – scratching   5 – swept   6 – explored

7 – museum   8 – hunters   9 – fashioned   10 – material

Chapter 4

Skim questions

Richard goes to meet the chef.

Richard meets the large cockroach from the previous night.

The chef gets spicy chili sauce in his face.

1 Scan questions

1 Elizabeth is studying Kokketti.

2 Richard uses a frying pan, a knife and bottle of chilli sauce.

3 They can't eat in the hotel restaurant because the chef had had an accident.

2 Key vocabulary

1 – c   2 – e   3 – h   4 – g   5 – a   6 – j   7 – b   8 – d   9 – k   10 – i

11 – f

3 Word partners

1 – c   2 – a   3 – h   4 – f   5 – b   6 – g   7 – e   8 – i   9 – d

4 Practice

a – interview   b – insist on   c – incredible   d – deafening   e – fell asleep

f – criminal

5 Summary

1 – look   2 – frying   3 – plates   4 – kill   5 – flew   6 – smashed

7 – escaped   8 – haircut   9 – insisted   10 – worried

Chapter 5

Skim questions

Richard dreams about the giant cockroach.

Richard drinks some Love Cola.

Elizabeth doesn't accept the job.

1 Scan questions

1 Richard talks to an antique dealer about football.

2 Richard wants to leave because of the cockroaches.

3 Elizabeth wants to leave because of the rats.

2 Key vocabulary

1 – c   2 – g   3 – l   4 – j   5 – i   6 – a   7 – k   8 – h   9 – b   10 – f

11 – d   12 – e

3 Word partners

1 – c   2 – g   3 – h   4 – i   5 – a   6 – d   7 – b   8 – j   9 – e   10 – f

4 Practice

a – mind   b – worship   c – dislike   d – off   e – bear   f – chasing   g – fake

5 Summary

1 – mind   2 – balcony   3 – roof   4 – dropped   5 – edge   6 – offered

7 – worshipped   8 – bear   9 – back   10 – squash

WORDLIST

Room Service

Chapter 1

Vocabulary

behaviour
bellboy
change
counter
impress
install
rail
suitable
tiled
tip

Word partners

carry on
conference facilities
fall off
fire brigade
flat screen
make a good impression
on average
reception area
shake hand
sort out

Chapter 2

Vocabulary

banknote
borrow
brilliant
dislike
guiltily
imagination
postponed
tanned
tough

Word partners

by the way
check in
conference delegate
get back
global warming
last minute flight
make a list
pick up
show you around
stone age

Chapter 3

Vocabulary

bench
complaint
crime
depressed
disinterested
foyer
furious
glitter
ignore
interrupt
moan
scan
spy
terrible

Word partners

a school of dolphins
arms crossed
backwards and forwards
break away
nice looking
in and out
put his arm around

Chapter 4

Vocabulary

blank
button
console
damage
demonstration
embarrassed
empty
knock
pocket
scream
shutters
stuck
tray

Word partners

at random
hands on hips
mess it up
multimedia projector
take place
turn it down
video conferencing
volume knob
watch in horror

Chapter 5

Vocabulary

accidentally
career
chaos
daft
misery
pretend
responsible
snap
squid

Word partners

book a flight
call you back
deal with
find out
in big trouble
pay her bill
pour through
spent the time
time off

Fish Legs

Chapter 1

Vocabulary

absurd
chambermaid
corridor
custard
healthy
poison
politely
seaweed
stuff
tip

Word partners

apart from
book a room
ghost hotel
half-board
past their sell-by date
shake his head
sun set
the end of the table

Chapter 2

Vocabulary

experience
lie
luckier
rub
rude
share
tap

Word partners

bump into
cross-legged
from time to time
powerful smell
rubbish bin
send it back
special feature
turn a corner

Chapter 3

Vocabulary

delicious
hairdryer
horrible
lobster
nod
shake
stiff
sunburnt
upset

Word partners

a telling off
as little as possible
come to life
join in
on the house
to hunt down
vacuum cleaning
win an argument

Chapter 4

Vocabulary

applaud
grab
reduce
shy
spotlights
stage
tender
transform
wander

Word partners

a roll of drums
at the end of the …
chocolates in a box
coach loads
cries of delight
high heels
pack tight together
sparkling costumes
surface differences

Chapter 5

Vocabulary

audience
clap
contribute
disgusting
hangover
hysterically
imitate
maracas
whisper

Word partners

a round of applause
a weak voice
have a turn
in time to the beat
side to side
stand in line
swing their hips
take off

Brooke's Hotel

Chapter 1

Vocabulary

advertising
blanket
cockroach
critic
grant
pre-book
rational
shine
terrified
tranquillizer

Word partners

advertising agency
air conditioned
bullet proof
good discount
one to another
run away
tropical heat

Chapter 2

Vocabulary

clump
courtyard
headquarters
lawn
mahogany
polished
reflect
rent
slogan
squeak

Word partners

bright sunshine
colonial building
cold and wet
cool and dark
great future
guide book
over the years
registration forms
turn into
wasting his time

Chapter 3

Vocabulary

attract
effective
explore
fold
illegal
panic
remind
scratching
spray
steady
sweep

Word partners

a brush and dustpan
brush their teeth
head hunters
in despair
insect spray
ivory bracelet
just in case
lay down

Chapter 4

Vocabulary

blow
criminal
deafening
determined
incredible
interview
nectar
pile
proud
refrigerators
stagger

Word partners

ground zero
fast asleep
frying pan
hot spicy sauce
insist on
ready for action
rub her eyes
proud of
threw herself

Chapter 5

Vocabulary

breathe
chase
dislike
fake
irritating
pant
sip
squashed
thumb
worship

Word partners

at peace with the world
burst into tears
can't bear
change your mind
from beginning to end
half dressed
on the edge of
slam shut
took his mind off

TRACKLIST